# HERALDRY

# UNDERSTANDING SIGNS & SYMBOLS

# HERALDRY

Stefan Oliver and Guy Croton

CHARTWELL
BOOKS, INC.

This edition published in 2012 by:
CHARTWELL BOOKS, INC.
A division of BOOK SALES, INC.
276 Fifth Avenue, Suite 206
New York, New York 10001
USA

ISBN-13: 978-0-7858-2966-9

QUMHBIB

A Quantum Book
This book is produced by
Quantum Publishing Ltd.,
6 Blundell Street
London N7 9BH

Design: Guy Croton
Managing Editor: Samantha Warrington
Assistant Editor: Jo Morley
Production Manager: Rohana Yusof
Publisher: Sarah Bloxham

Printed in China by Midas Printing International Ltd.

# CONTENTS

# INTRODUCTION

Heraldry is as alive today as it has always been. Few people can fail to be impressed by the eye-catching delights of its insignia. The magnificence of its colorful array can be seen all around us—on public buildings, in churches, on flags, on documents—just about everywhere.

Heraldic symbols and devices provide a decorative and attractive display while offering a permanent symbol of ownership and individuality in a unique and ever-lasting way. This ancient art and science carries the long-cherished traditions of chivalry, honor, and duty into the 21st century. In this age of mass production and computerized conformity we are all subject to the powerful influences of the internet, television, and advertising. The production of consumer items is in the hands of fewer and fewer, bigger and bigger international corporations.

The clothes and cars that we buy, the houses in which we live, and the foods that we eat, are becoming more and more standardized.

As a result, people are becoming increasingly interested in finding ways—no matter how small—in which to assert their own personalities. Heraldry is able to offer people a symbol that is legally personal to them, one which they can pass on to their descendants, which may be used in a great variety of ways to decorate their property in a dignified fashion, and which carries significant historical links into modern times.

Today people are coming to understand that heraldry is not simply a subject of medieval history, but is as alive and meaningful in our modern world as it has ever been. Unhappily, misconceptions about heraldry—many of them deliberately sustained by people who wish to wrap the subject in mystery—have tended to confuse people and put them off the subject entirely. People fear and deride things that they

do not understand. Heraldry, being an ancient subject, has customs and a language which are unfamiliar to us and which tend to confuse and hide its true meaning. It is versed in an ancient, though simple and fairly limited, terminology that tends to mystify those who are unwilling to learn it. People are, however, beginning to accept technical jargons as they become more widely used in industry and technology, so that this barrier is happily being rapidly removed.

There is, unfortunately, a quite unjustified social resistance to heraldry, fostered by those who do not understand the subject. The origins of heraldry lay in the desire for personal identification. It is true that in medieval times the people who sought this identification were of a high rank in society and that heraldry became an honor. It is true, also, that it has remained a mark of honor down to our own day. One of the great strengths of our society, however, is that this honor is not confined to a handful of people born into privilege, but is available to anyone who by his own effort or good fortune has been able to take the steps needed to become a "top person." There are those who feel that an honor should not be inherited by succeeding generations. But who, having earned for him or herself an honor, or a fortune, would not leave it to their children? The proposition that anyone in this position would divest themselves of everything and tell their children to start from the beginning is preposterous. Let those who complain about the unfairness of inherited wealth or honor set about obtaining for themselves that which they

ABOVE: Shields on a tomb in Lincoln cathedral (c. 1340); the arms of Bohun (*left*) are azure between six lioncells or a bend argent cotized or. The shield on the right is Hastings quartering de valence.

BELOW: The arms of the Bishop Goldwell Chantry in Norwich Cathedral; argent a chief or overall a lion rampant ermine.

The splendid armorial tomb of Sir Richard Mompesson in Salisbury Cathedral.

An ornately decorated archway on the south side of the presbytery of Norwich Cathedral. An heraldic description of the shield repeated at either end, would be: "Boleyn-Argent a chevron gules between three bulls' heads sable." After reading this book hopefully you will be able to understand such a description at a glance and, if you wished, could sketch the shield, sight unseen.

purport to despise. However, also let those who have inherited an honor, be it an heraldic device or an ancient title, remember that they are the living representatives of the one to whom the honor was originally granted and that it is their duty to preserve and foster its worth.

At first sight, a large "achievement of arms," dazzling though it may be in its brilliant colors and array, presents an incomprehensible mass of fine detail that is bewildering to the uninitiated. And if they look up the achievement in a book,

they may be baffled by what they read and left with more questions than answers. What is it all about? Where did it all come from? Why is it so apparently incomprehensible?

This short book cannot unravel all the detail that has accumulated over many centuries; nor can it provide all the answers. The hope is that it will start readers along the path that will lead to a more scholarly and comprehensive study, once their enthusiasm has been kindled and their curiosity rewarded with a basic understanding.

# CHAPTER 1

# KNIGHTS AND CHIVALRY

# THE RISE OF HERALDRY

HERALDRY HAS ITS ORIGINS IN MEDIEVAL WARFARE, AND STEMS FROM THE WARRIOR'S PRIMITIVE DESIRE TO DISPLAY AN EMBLEM IN BATTLE TO STRENGTHEN HIS OWN MORALE AND STRIKE TERROR INTO THE HEART OF HIS ENEMY. IT BECAME AN IMPORTANT SYSTEM OF IDENTIFICATION AND THRIVES WORLDWIDE TO THIS DAY.

All over the world and all through history examples of this kind of decoration can be found. As soon as man was able to grasp the advantage to be had from using a weapon to hit or pierce his foe, he had also to develop a shield to protect him from retaliation. The large surface thus provided was the ideal vehicle for military decoration. Those early devices were not thought to be hereditary and so they were, really, pre-heraldic. It is doubtful whether those devices were permanent; and a person may have used different ones on different occasions. It is known, for example, that the Norman knights did not later use the devices with which, if the evidence of the Bayeux tapestry is accurate, they fought at Hastings. By then, however, it was already necessary, because of armor in the form of chain mail and helmets that covered a large part of the face, for leaders and knights to have devices on their shields, flags, and standards by which they could be recognized.

The great feudal overlords also found it desirable to have some form of recognizable symbol with which they could authenticate documents and instructions that they issued to their largely illiterate subjects; and so there came into use seals that depicted the overlord on his horse, in battle array, with a shield bearing his devices.

Church establishments also used seals, with a picture of the bishop or abbot, as appropriate, engraved upon them. All the land in Europe was nominally in the hands of kings, who rewarded their followers by giving them land. For the most part kings were wise enough not

to give large, single blocks of land to anybody, thus diminishing the risk of powerful territorial magnates setting themselves up as rivals to the throne. Landowners usually held their estates in scattered parcels, and since they were unable to make frequent visits to all of them, the need for seals was greatly increased. Seals, carried by the lords' messengers, were marks of authority, badges of identification.

## KNIGHT FEES

Landowners held their land on the condition that they provide knights to ride to battle when the king required them. This was known as "knight fee." Only very wealthy landowners could supply a sufficient number of knights from their own resources and so they, in turn, would grant some of their land to lesser knights in return for knight fee to ride for the king or for themselves, as required. The more land one acquired, the greater one's power and influence and the more knights one could put at one's own or the king's service.

In the recurrent feudal wars of the time, when knights rode all over the country to fight on one side or another, it was necessary that each of them should wear a badge or symbol of the lord to whom he belonged and on whose side he was fighting. Thus kings and lords adopted some simple object as a badge to distinguish their followers in the field. This practice gained wide acceptance in western Europe, during the Crusades of the 11th, 12th, and 13th centuries. The Holy Land, the birthplace of Christianity, was overrun by the

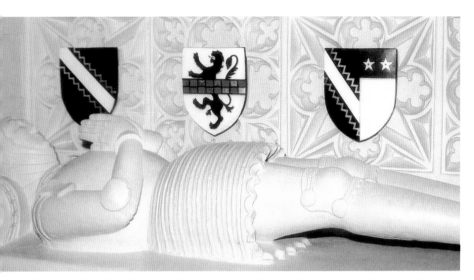

ABOVE: The tomb of Sir William Clopton, displaying (*left to right*) his paternal arms, the arms of his mother Elizabeth Mylde, and his own arms joined on the same shield with his first wife Marjory, and his second wife, also Marjory.

BELOW: Detail of the Bayeux Tapestry depicting the Battle of Hastings between King Harold of England and the invading forces of Duke William of Normandy. The devices that the figures display are not thought to be heraldic because the same figures wear different emblems in different episodes shown in the tapestry, and the descendants of those same individuals did not display the same emblems.

Muslim Turks, who cut off Christians' access to it. The Pope called on all Christian leaders to take up arms and liberate the Holy Lands. Numerous expeditions were mounted from western Europe, some successful, some not (and some bizarre in the extreme). Men set forth under the sign of the Cross, emblazoned on their cloaks, shields, and banners, in different colors and different forms for each country and large group. Their swords were made in the shape of crosses and engraved with pious emblems and inscriptions. Thus the idea of a collective badge to identify a group took universal hold throughout Europe for the first time in history.

## ACCUMULATION OF LAND

Any ambitious lord sought to increase the amount of his land. One of the best ways was to marry a lady who held land in her own right,

either because she was a widow or because she was her father's heiress. As the number of young men who died in battle or from disease was high, and the number of wives who died in childbirth considerable, there was ample opportunity by judicious marriages to acquire large estates. A new husband would mark his authority over newly acquired lands by displaying on his seal the armorial bearings of this new land. This practice meant that the mounted figure on the seals was soon dropped in favor of one shield showing all the arms belonging to the different people who had formerly held the land. Some seals also had the main arms engraved on a shield in the middle and the new ones on smaller shields around the outside. The passing of arms from one person to another in this way inevitably led to their being passed from father to son. In these ways, heraldry as we know it today, was born.

Shown here is the seal of Southwold. The borough has never had a grant of arms.

Elizabeth Talbot (*left*), daughter of John Talbot, Earl of Shrewsbury and wife of John de Mowbray, the last Mowbray Duke of Norfolk, and Elizabeth Tilney (*right*), daughter of Sir Francis Tilney and wife of Thomas Howard, Duke of Norfolk. Each displays her own arms on her dress and her husband's arms on her cloak.

The Duke of Normandy, now William the Conqueror, granting land in England
to his supporters, who are depicted bearing the arms later attributed to them.

BELOW: Sir William Clopton, son of Sir Thomas Clopton. The ermine spot on the arms he displays on his surcoat distinguishes him from his father.

ABOVE: Ann Denston, in Long Melford Church, Suffolk. She wears her own arms on her dress and those of her husband on her cloak.

## THE IDEALS OF CHIVALRY

In medieval times land was farmed by people who paid a rent in kind, either as part of their crop or in service to their lord, who was thus free to devote himself to other pursuits. Much of his energy was devoted to military activities, either on his own behalf or on that of his overlord or king. With the example of the crusades before them, young men prepared themselves by prayer, fasting, and ritual to join a company of knights and to lead a life in the military service of others. So the high ideals of courage, perseverance, and generosity to others were bred into them at an early age. In order to acquire skill in battle, they spent many hours in practice combat. This led to friendly competitions and the idea of the tournament was born.

## THE TOURNAMENT

Knights from all over Europe "went from one tournament to the next, trying their skill, displaying their prowess, and winning such prizes and favor as they could." Tournaments were great social events and therefore occasions for brilliant and exaggerated heraldic display. The contestants hung up their shields outside their lodgings when they arrived so that everyone would know who was in town. People came from miles around to see the spectacle and visit the accompanying fair. On the day of the tournament itself, the contestants displayed their armorial bearings on their shields, their coats of arms, and their horse trappings; they painted them on tents and marquees, on banners and flags, on anything that they could find to make a splendid display. They fashioned ornate crests on their helmets, made from wood or softened leather, representing animals, birds, and all kinds of devices. Their shields were carried around the arena, for all to see, by pages dressed in costumes of exotic and fierce animals. The spectators and their wives wore their armorial bearings emblazoned on their cloaks, dresses, and surcoats. The whole event was a stunning pageant and carnival. The proceedings were presided over by the heralds, who acted as

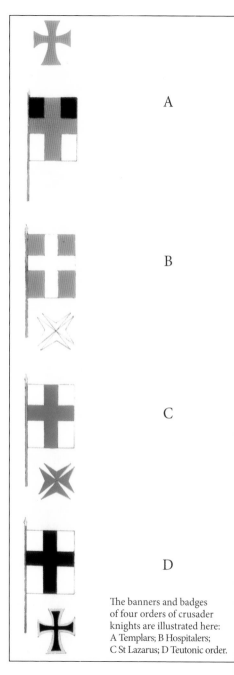

A

B

C

D

The banners and badges of four orders of crusader knights are illustrated here: A Templars; B Hospitalers; C St Lazarus; D Teutonic order.

Sir Tristan, fighting in a melée at court, watched by the queen and her ladies. Sir Tristan was reckoned to be one of the five "dangerous knights," second only to Sir Lancelot. Here he is fighting Sir Palomedes, who later became his friend.

After the melée, or tournament, fell out of favor, considered too dangerous, the joust grew in popularity amongst the aristocracy. Single combat could be fought on foot or on horseback with a variety of weapons and usually ended with only serious bruising. This 13th-Century illustration shows combatants in action. During a joust a knight, unseated from his mount by a blunted lance (top), would lose the contest, while in a sword fight the outclassed knight surrendered his weapon to his victor (bottom).

masters of ceremonies and referees and ensured that things ran smoothly.

The importance of the tournament to the culture of medieval knights cannot be overestimated. It provided an arena for the display of knightly virtues: *prouesse* in the combat; *courtoisie* to the watching and judging ladies; *largesse* to the crowds of minstrels, heralds, armorers, squires, and assorted hangers on. Also on display were knightly qualities such as the *franchise* and *debonnaireté* with which a knight should conduct himself in triumph and disaster (qualities that developed into the European gentlemen's sense of fair play), and the *pité* he should exercise to his defeated opponents.

It was regarded as a crucial training ground for young knights to practice handling their horses and weapons, the tactics of attack and defense, and of coordinating their actions with a team of companions, who would in real battle form a military unit. It was an opportunity for knights to win praise and glory, and to find employment with great lords who attended the tournaments and frequently recruited talented knights there. To this end the activities of the heralds were of vital importance, as they recorded the names and arms of those who took part in tournaments and the deeds they achieved. It was also a splendid occasion for sexual display. It is clear that ladies played a variety of active

A detail from a military roll compiled in 1448—a jousting tournament. While the heraldic arms worn by jousting combatants did not quite serve the vital purpose that they did on the battlefield, they were still important in enabling the audience to identify the competing knights. The latter would also make much of the fact that their unique liveries told everyone else just who was in town.

roles in the tournament; from hosting them, to encouraging individual knights, who competed wearing their "favor" (a sleeve or other token), judging performances (before this role was taken over by heralds), giving prizes and, on occasion, being the prize themselves.

A knight could win considerable sums at tournaments, if he was successful; conversely, of course, he could also lose money. There can be no doubt that the prospect of winning valuable horses, armor, and ransoms contributed to the extreme popularity of tournaments all over Europe and throughout the period. It was possible for a knight who was good at tourneying to travel from tournament to

tournament, accumulating a considerable fortune as well as a formidable reputation. There were also knights for whom the sport was an addiction, who returned time after time to tournaments although their losses might reduce them to bankruptcy and ruin.

The expenses of tourneying, though great, were much less serious than the physical dangers to which knights were inevitably exposed. In their early days, tournaments were fairly unregulated free-for-alls and they were so violent that the only distinction between them and a real battle was the fact that they were acknowledged to be waged in sport. Over time, they became regulated so that the danger was less extreme.

# DISPLAY OF HERALDRY

The illustration on the opposite page is imaginary and serves to demonstrate the ways in which the medieval knights displayed their different devices. Tournaments, as well as providing important training for knights in battle, were also major social occasions and it was very important to put on a good show. They were also occasions when many grudges and grievances were settled and so it was essential that the protagonists conducted themselves in great style.

Lord Stafford is depicted on his war horse with his heraldic device or (gold) a chevron gules (red) emblazoned on his surcoat, his horse's caparisons, and on the head shield of his mount. Upon the rein trimming is displayed his badge, the well-known Stafford knot. Atop his helmet is his crest of a swan, with a ducal crown. A page dressed in his livery colors stands holding his lance in readiness. The lance has a pennant, hanging point down when the lance is being used. The page has the badge of his master emblazoned on his chest as does the page holding his master's banner, ready to bear it round the arena before the Lord as he makes his entry. The personal herald, waiting to announce his master, displays the badge on his hat and wears a tabard of his master's arms. Lord Stafford's pavilion, which serves as a changing room and a store for all his accoutrements, is also made of striped material representing the two main colors of his arms. It is decorated with his knot badge and his standard flies from its center pole. This long flag whose main purpose is to display his heraldic devices, is made in his livery colors and decorated with his crest and badge. At the hoist it has the cross of St. George. Two pages stand ready to display his shield to the crowd. They are dressed as his supporters in the costumes of two white swans gorged with a ducal crown.

Lord Stafford's wife, Phillipa, daughter of Thomas Beauchamp, wears a dress of her paternal arms and a mantel of those of her husband. In the illustration, she is handing him a cup. Lord Stafford's daughter, Catherine, who was married to Michael de la Pole, Duke of Suffolk, similarly wears her father's arms as her gown and her husband's arms upon her cloak.

If all the knights and their ladies and retainers disported themselves in this way—as historians believe to have been the case—the great tournaments must have been a riotous display of color, costume, and pageantry as the excitement of the tournament combined with the hurly burly of the accompanying fair, the vendors selling their wares, the jugglers, the tumblers, the fortune tellers, and the booths selling spitted pig and other foods. The troubadours and the ale tents; the ringing of the blacksmith's forge as he repaired damaged armor; the games of chance and skill; and the revelry going on far into the night. The event must have drawn people from far and wide and in an era when there was little entertainment, it must have been the highlight of the year.

Through all this festive mêlée the heralds had to hold court. It was their job to make sure that no one appeared in the lists displaying the arms of another. They had to organize and marshall the events, adjudicate on questions of heraldry, and grant arms to those aspirants deemed worthy. The great lords of the day sometimes granted arms to their followers or retainers that were different versions or allusive to their own as a mark of approval, thanks, or favor. The heralds had to record these, check that they were unique, and adjudicate in any dispute. A great tournament, when knights were gathered from far and wide, gave them just such an opportunity.

Hugh Lord Stafford awaiting his entry into the lists at a tournament.

# THE HERALD'S ROLE

HERALDS HAVE BEEN EMPLOYED BY KINGS AND GREAT LANDOWNERS FROM VERY EARLY TIMES. THEY WERE PRINCIPALLY DEPLOYED AS MESSENGERS AND AMBASSADORS AND ARE BELIEVED TO HAVE COME ORIGINALLY FROM THE RANKS OF ROAMING TROUBADOURS AND MINSTRELS, WHO WENT FROM ONE PLACE TO ANOTHER WITH THEIR SONGS AND TALES.

It seems clear that when they were acting as messengers or ambassadors, heralds were free to come and go as they pleased, even across national frontiers. They wore a tabard emblazoned with their master's arms while on "official duty" and this was supposed to guarantee them protection. An attack on a herald who was wearing his master's arms was equivalent to an attack on the master. Most powerful lords had land scattered about all over the country. Heralds were, therefore, constantly traveling and meeting other heralds and other lords; in this way they soon began to gather considerable knowledge of the armorial bearings of other people, particularly those immediate neighbors of their lords. This gave rise to their second important function, that of staff officer in battle.

## THE HERALD'S ROLE
## AS STAFF OFFICER

In medieval times many disputes were settled by force. Before embarking upon a dispute over borders with your neighbor, however, it was important to know how many knights he could put in the field against you. Heralds could easily discover this. During a battle itself they were also able to tell their lord, by recognizing the arms, who the opponents were, how many knights they could put into the field, and what men they had under their command. They also reported who had left or joined the battle and what forces they had taken away or added. This last function was very important, since many of the combatants were involved only for what

they could obtain for themselves; expected allies sometimes held back from the fray and joined it only when it was clear which side was going to win—not always the side with whom they had started out!

Heralds quite often had to decide who had won a battle. At the Battle of Agincourt, the French and English heralds watched the day's events together and in the evening reported to King Henry of England that the "day was his."

## THE IMPORTANCE OF
## CAPTURE AND RANSOM

Another important function was the identifying of captives. Important people were held hostage for the ransom that could be gained and ordinary people were put to death. It was obviously necessary to get this right! Heralds also had the unenviable task of identifying the dead. This presented no great difficulty when men fought largely on foot and wore chain mail with open helmets made of iron. The slain could be easily recognized. Knights used to wear over their chain mail a long, loose, padded coat, made of tough material, to help protect them from sword cuts, and they adopted the practice of painting their armorial bearings on these. This was called coat armor, or coat of arms, and is the derivation of the phrase, coat of arms. If the face of the slain was not recognizable, it was possible to identify him by his coat of arms. When, in later years, knights started to wear plate armor and closed helmets, it was impossible to recognize anyone except by his coat of arms; the heralds therefore insisted that

# THE EARLY HERALDS

THIS MODERN IMPRESSION OF WHAT A MEDIEVAL HERALD WOULD HAVE LOOKED LIKE IS BORNE OUT BY COUNTLESS HISTORICAL DOCUMENTS AND ATTESTATIONS. THE EARLY HERALD'S ROLE WAS ACTUALLY VERY STRAIGHTFORWARD, AS WAS SPLENDIDLY DEMONSTRATED IN CHRÉTIEN DE TROYES' POEM *LANCELOT*:

At the great tournament which takes place toward the end of the poem, Lancelot, who has attended in borrowed armor in order not to be recognized, is resting in his lodgings and has left his plain vermilion shield outside the door, as the custom was at the time (*c*.1170–1190). Along comes a herald-at-arms, looking at all the shields so that he will know who is taking part in the tournament later on. He does not recognize Lancelot's borrowed shield, so he steps into the house and instantly recognizes Lancelot himself. Lancelot forbids him to reveal his name to anyone, upon which

the herald hastens away, shouting out "Now there has come one who will take the measure!" This herald is clearly not a very grand or dignified person, because Chrétien mentions that he has left his robe and shoes behind in a tavern as a pledge, meaning that he has no money and the tavern-keeper will hold onto the robe and shoes until he can find someone to pay his bill. So the herald looks for a patron among the knights— someone who will reward him with knightly *largesse* for the service of crying his fame (even if, as in this case, he must not mention the knight's name).

Heralds in attendance at the funeral of the wife of Lord Lumley,
bearing banners of the arms of her forebears.

knights continue to wear a short surcoat, with
their arms painted on them, so that mistakes
could be avoided.

When knights charged into battle on their
great war horses, wielding huge axes, lances,
and swords, the force of the impact must have
been terrible. Not only was it a question of
identifying the dead, but quite literally a matter
of finding all the right parts of the slain body!
The use of arms emblazoned on everything,
including the crest of the helmet, enabled the
heralds to perform this grisly task. The clash
of a couple of hundred knights, charging full
pelt at one another and wielding every kind of
dismembering weapon, must have been sheer
bedlam. No wonder so many knight effigies
are shown wearing armor—it was probably so
battered that it could not be removed.

## HERALDS AND TOURNAMENTS

Because of their knowledge of armorial
bearings, heralds were required to recognize
and announce contestants at tournaments and
it soon became their responsibility to organize
and referee these events. Because of the social
nature of the event and the desire by everyone
to put on a good display, heralds were needed
to advise would-be contestants about the choice
of armorial bearings that they could use. They
were able to make sure that no one chose the
arms of another that were already in use.

People came to them for advice on heraldic
matters and they began to keep lists of all the
armorial bearings used at different tournaments,
gatherings, and battles and of the people who
bore them. These lists were collected on long
rolls of parchment and were called rolls of arms,

At tournaments, it was the herald's job to ensure that no knight should inadvertently wear the colors of another and generally to keep the contestants in order and fully apprised of the latest heraldic developments.

Heralds performed many valuable roles in medieval society, dealing with a huge variety of people.

or simply rolls. Many of these have survived and they provide a valuable record of early heraldry. Because the heralds became so involved in the study and recording of coats of arms and in advising and adjudicating on matters relating to them, the business became known as heraldry. In England the heralds were incorporated by royal charter in 1484. Since people continued to assume coats of arms, without having them registered and recorded at the College of Arms, disputes frequently arose over who was the actual owner of a coat of arms. Consequently, the heralds were required to tour the country and record all coats of arms, so that they could be registered and disputes be settled. Most of these visitations, as they were called, took place in the 16th century. They form the basis upon which ownership of

arms is proved today. The records, however, are not complete, for those were stormy times in England, and in some instances people were unable to answer the call of the visiting herald, because they were confined to their place of residence. The motive of the visitation may often have been political and not strictly for the well-being of heraldry. It was a worthwhile exercise for sovereigns to record their supporters and disqualify those who could not support them.

## THE ROLE OF THE HERALDS TODAY

Heralds still have important duties as officers of the crown, and apart from these duties are very active in heraldic affairs. Interest in heraldic matters is steadily increasing and there are now

A roll of arms of the Lord of the Manor of Long Melford Hall in Suffolk, dating from 1044.

more matters needing their attention than ever before. Their work falls into three categories.

*Confirming arms*
There are still people eager to have confirmed to them arms that they have always used, but for which they have to prove a right of descent. The heralds are glad to help in this work, which involves a lot of patient genealogical research, since, despite the records of centuries, a mass of detail still needs to be recorded.

*Granting arms*
Any worthy person may apply for a grant of arms and the heralds will be pleased to steer the applicant safely through the process. For more on the granting of arms, see pages 30–31.

*Devising arms*
The heralds of Great Britain have jurisdiction only over subjects of the crown. Although many people of British origin who are citizens of other countries wish to register coats of arms or varieties of arms belonging to their families to show their ancient lineage, the heralds cannot grant arms to them. They can, however, following the proper searches, "devise" arms that could be used, and register them in their records so that they will not be issued to others.

The heralds take great care to ensure that any arms, crests, supporters, mottoes, badges, or standards are unique to the grantees they are dealing with. This is the point of the exercise. Heraldry exists to identify individuals. There is no such thing as "arms of a name."

# GRANTEES OF ARMS

HERALDIC DEVICES ARE PASSED DOWN FROM ONE GENERATION TO THE NEXT. WHEN A SON COMES OF AGE, HE IS ENTITLED TO DISPLAY HIS FATHER'S COAT OF ARMS, BEARING SOME SMALL MARK OF DIFFERENCE SO THAT IT IS POSSIBLE TO TELL ONE FROM THE OTHER. OTHER RULES APPLY TO THE ARMS OF OTHER FAMILY MEMBERS.

If someone is not in a position to inherit a coat of arms in the traditional way, they can apply for a grant of arms. Few nations today still retain formal bodies that grant arms to individuals, but it is possible in England, which has the oldest heraldic authority in the world, the English College of Arms.

Any person receiving a grant of heraldic arms is known as a "grantee of arms." In order to apply for a grant, one must make a formal request for the right to bear them, in the form of what is known as a "petition." The steps required to make a petition are roughly these:

• First of all, it is necessary to check that an aspirant "armiger" (bearer of arms) is not entitled to an existing coat of arms. That is to say, that no hereditary right to a coat of arms already exists.

• If the applicant is indeed not entitled to an extant coat of arms, it is then necessary to consider with them a possible design and to check that the design in question is not already held by someone else.

• Once it has been established that the design is unique and it has been approved by all parties, it can be granted to the applicant as the sole right of him and his legal descendants.

• As well as private individuals, many commercial undertakings and corporate institutions apply for grants of arms.

Although anyone of English nationality or descent is entitled to petition the English heralds for a coat of arms, it is by no means an inalienable right that arms should be granted to them. It is entirely at the discretion of the heralds as to whether someone is deemed fit to receive arms. The English College of Arms applies certain criteria that are known only to them, and any applicant who does not meet those criteria in full may be refused arms.

At the time of writing, the cost of a patent of arms in England is roughly $5,000 (£3,300). Of course, the size of this fee might deter some people who otherwise have a strong interest in making a petition for arms, although to many the very idea of having to pay for the privilege in the first place is repugnant. However, it is unlikely that just being able to pay the fee without conscience will be enough to secure a successful result. It is also important to be of proven good character and, ideally, to be as "eminent" as possible in one's field of activity.

One important thing to note in all this is that there are many rogue organizations and websites that purport to sell genuine coats of arms for a fixed price, with pretty much no questions asked. However, the notion that such arms are legitimate and valid is a deliberate misconception perpetrated by those who would exploit the ignorant for base profit. Knowledge of the outlines of heraldry protects people from being persuaded to buy a shield of arms with their name on it, on the false understanding that it might be theirs.

ABOVE: The University of Newcastle's beautiful grant of arms celebrates the university's emergence as an autonomous institution in 1965.

BELOW: In addition, the university holds the 1974 grant of arms for the Newcastle College of Education, an institution which amalgamated with the University of Newcastle in 1989.

# ECCLESIASTICAL HERALDRY

H ERALDIC-LIKE DEVICES HAVE BEEN USED BY CHURCHES SINCE THE BEGINNING OF CHRISTIANITY. FOR CENTURIES IN MANY DIFFERENT PARTS OF THE WORLD, ECCLESIASTICAL ESTABLISHMENTS HAVE BEEN GRANTED LAND BY THE SOVEREIGN OR—THROUGH PIETY OR THE DESIRE TO EXPIATE SINS—BY LANDOWNERS.

For this reason, since the earliest times the church has had to fulfill the role of lord of the manor. Consequently, ecclesiastical establishments have needed to use seals, badges, and other devices in order to identify themselves and their retainers. These devices developed along heraldic lines over the centuries and, although different denominations have different traditions, some general comments can be made about this alternative form of heraldry.

## EPISCOPAL HERALDRY

A bishop, who has authority over a number of priests in an area called a diocese, can, like the holder of a civic office, impale his personal arms—if he has them—with the official arms of his diocese. He places the diocesan arms on the dexter (right) side of his shield and his own on the sinister (left) side (see page 44). On the Continent it is quite common for a bishop to quarter his arms with those of his see. He may also place a miter over his shield and display behind it a crozier, or two in saltire, or an episcopal staff, as an emblem of his episcopal authority.

A number of terms in episcopal heraldry deserve attention and explanation:

## CROZIER

This ceremonial staff, based on the shepherd's crook, symbolizes the episcopal authority of a bishop. It has a crook to gather in the lost, a stout staff to hold up the weak, and a point to goad the reluctant! For centuries this has been the ultimate symbol of ecclesiastical authority.

## EPISCOPAL HAT

This is a flat hat with a wide brim, a shallow crown, and pendant tassels. It is used in different colors and with different numbers of tassels to indicate the rank of the cleric.

## EPISCOPAL STAFF

This has a function similar to that of a crozier, but has a cross (of varying types) on the head instead of a crook. Cardinals, who are of a higher rank than bishops, can display over their arms a red hat with tassels, fifteen on each side (see the illustration on the opposite page). If they are also bishops, they can show under their hat a miter and a crozier.

## MITERS

The miter can take a variety of forms within two broad categories—completely plain, "miter simplex," or heavily decorated and jeweled, "miter preciosa." Instead of displaying a miter shown over his arms, a bishop may show a green episcopal hat with green tassels hanging down on both sides of the shield (see the illustration on page 35).

As a matter of style, the Catholic church now favors an achievement of arms showing the episcopal arms with an ecclesiastical hat placed above and a staff placed behind. Anglican churches place a gold miter and crossed croziers behind the arms. Eastern churches use the eastern forms of miter and staff.

## PAPAL HERALDRY

Popes, like other high dignitaries of the church, have frequently used the horsehead-shaped

The arms of a cardinal traditionally display the red cardinal's hat with 15 tassels on each side.

shield, which looks less military and therefore is more suited to a man of God. For the same reason, it is not now felt appropriate for a cleric of any rank to display a crest and helm; hence the adoption of different orders of the clerical hat. Papal heraldry has also adopted other symbols, as outlined below:

## TIARA

The tiara is the triple crown of the pope. The shape of the hat on which the three crowns are placed has long been considered an emblem of liberty and the three crowns are said to symbolize the pope's supremacy over the church militant, the church penitent, and the church triumphant. They also symbolize his three roles as priest, pastor, and teacher.

## CROSSED KEYS OF ST. PETER

These are always shown with the tiara as a symbol of the papacy and are commonly placed on a red shield. A pope will place the tiara over the papal arms and the crossed keys behind his personal arms. The keys symbolize the power to bind or lock in and to set free or loose.

## OTHER ECCLESIASTICAL SYMBOLS
## UMBALINO OR PAVILION

This is shown as an umbrella, or tent, with a red and gold striped cover. It is used as the emblem of a basilica in the Catholic church. With crossed keys it is used as the emblem of authority of the cardinal in charge ("Camerlengo") in an interregnum between popes. When placed with the crossed keys behind, it has been used by Italian families in association with their arms to indicate that they have had a pope in the family.

## PALLIUM

This is a band of cloth, worn about the shoulders, charged with black crosses and two pendant strips. It is a symbol of authority given by the pope to an archbishop, who cannot commence his office until he receives it. It is displayed wherever it is possible to arrange it satisfactorily with the achievement. It may be found as a charge on a shield, as it is in the Archdiocese of Canterbury.

## ROSARY

This string of beads, ten and one repeated five times, is used to count repeated contemplative prayers. It is sometimes found arranged around a shield. A rosary was normally used by a knight who had taken religious vows.

A statue of St. Peter the Apostle holding his famous crossed keys to the gates of heaven, photographed beside a door on the western facade of Isaak Cathedral in St. Petersburg, Russia.

The arms of the Anglican Bishop of Ely. The gold miter is in the Anglican style, but in this case there are no crossed croziers, which are usually displayed behind the arms.

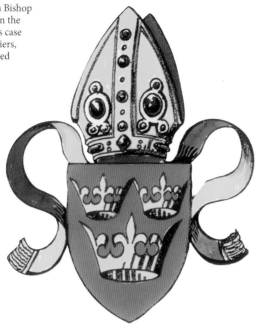

The arms of a bishop often display a green episcopal hat with tassels instead of a miter.

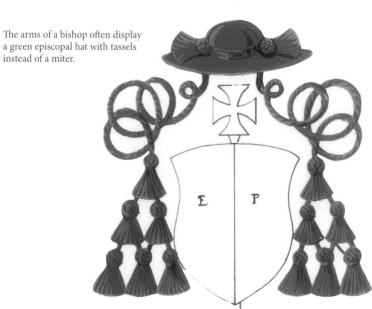

# ORDERS OF CHIVALRY AND ENTITLEMENT TO ARMS

FOR CENTURIES IT HAS BEEN THE CUSTOM OF SOVEREIGNS TO INSTIGATE ORDERS OF CHIVALRY THAT HONOR THE NATION'S MOST DISTINGUISHED MEN AND, IN MORE RECENT TIMES, WOMEN. THESE ORDERS HAVE EMBLEMS THAT THE MEMBERS ARE OBLIGED TO WEAR AND WHICH APPEAR ON THEIR ACHIEVEMENTS OF ARMS.

Practice in this area varies widely from country to country and it is beyond the scope of this book to go into the subject in great detail. However, here are details of some of the main chivalric emblems and badges of honor:

## CIRCLET
European knights of an order often place a circlet around a shield. It is usually shown with a motto, as, for example, in the British Order of the Garter, which is blue with a gold edge and buckle and has the motto, "Honi soit qui mal y pense"—"Evil be to he who evil thinks."

## CHAIN
This is usually called a collar, a gold chain worn around the arms, with the emblems of the order in alternate links and the badge of the order pendant, as, for example, in the Swedish Order of the Seraphim. People may display collars of more than one order. Care should be taken with chains, as some officers of state also display a chain.

## BADGE
The badge of an order is displayed by lower-ranking members of the order on a riband, below the shield.

## RELIGIOUS ORDERS OF CHIVALRY
These are survivors of the crusades, when knights joined the military and hospital orders to fight for the holy lands and care for the sick and wounded soldiers and pilgrims. Some of these continue to exist for philanthropic purposes. They have their own arms and badges, known as crosses.

Grandmasters can show the arms of the order on their shields as a chief or quartering. Knights and dames of the order display the cross of their order behind the shield. Members can hang the cross of the order on a riband of the order below the shield.

## ENTITLEMENT TO ARMS
Anyone may apply for a new grant of arms, but a person is entitled to existing arms only if he can prove that he is descended in the male line from someone to whom a grant of arms has previously been made. Some countries permit people to assume arms at will, but there is then no guarantee that the arms are unique.

Heraldry is essentially a European phenomenon. Because heraldic authorities in Europe have jurisdiction only over citizens of their own country, anyone wishing to enquire into their heraldic status should of course apply to the authority in his own country.

In the New World the position is slightly different. Many of the peoples of those countries are of European ancestry. If a person wishes to prove his right to an existing coat of arms, he must apply to his country of origin or that of his ancestors. If he seeks a new coat of arms, he must apply to his own country.

A vintage engraving of the Insignia of the Order of the Garter,
taken from the Trousset encyclopedia (1886–1891).

# CHAPTER 2

# THE HERALD'S
# RULES

# THE BLAZON AND BLAZONRY

MANY PEOPLE ARE BAFFLED BY THE CURIOUS LANGUAGE THAT ATTENDS HERALDRY, WHICH IN ENGLISH-SPEAKING COUNTRIES IS LARGELY DERIVED FROM MEDIEVAL NORMAN FRENCH. COLLECTIVELY THE TERMINOLOGY IS KNOWN AS THE "BLAZON" OR "BLAZONRY," WHICH IS ACTUALLY EASY TO LEARN ONCE THE BASIC PRINCIPLES HAVE BEEN MASTERED.

## THE LANGUAGE OF HERALDRY

One of the things that puts people off a study of heraldry is the language—students of the subject constantly come up against terms that they simply do not understand. Like many specialist subjects, heraldry has its own technical language, or jargon, that must be learned. As modern life becomes more and more technical, specialist jargons are entering more and more into everyday language; as a result, people are showing less resistance to the jargon of heraldry than they once did. In this way the circumstances of modern life are removing an obstacle to the study of what is, after all, a medieval science.

Heraldry had its origins in western Europe at a time when the predominant language was Norman French and some of that language survives in the heraldic terms that are employed today. There are not, however, very many such terms surviving; those that do, chiefly concern the basic matters of design and color. The simplest way to learn these terms is to use them; so they are gradually introduced throughout this book and explained as they appear.

## THE BLAZON

A written description of a coat of arms may at first appear to make little sense; but once you become used to the language and the way that it is set out, you will find that a well-written description is a masterpiece of concision that should enable any artist to draw correctly everything that is displayed on the shield. This description is known as the "blazon."

To "blazon" a coat of arms is to describe it in words. To "emblazon" it, is to paint or draw it in full color.

The blazon always follows a set pattern in heraldry, with very strict rules being applied. In the following chapters we will consider what might be painted on a shield in the same order, but first let us examine some of the language and precise terms which define that process.

## BASIC SHIELD DESIGNS

On a shield, any "charge" or decoration can be combined with any other in any number of different ways in order to make up a coat of arms. In the early days of heraldry, many designs of shield were very basic indeed, and in fact some shields displayed only a plain color or the simplest of patterns (see the illustration on the opposite page).

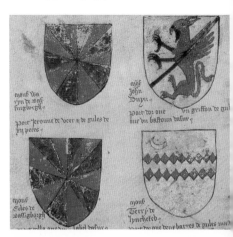

ABOVE: Ancient examples of coats of arms bearing a plain tincture only are (from left to right) those of Bruget of Normandy ("argent"), Berrington of Chester ("azure"), and the Duke of Brittany ("ermine").

LEFT: The Carlisle Roll of 1334 lists King Edward III of England's commanders and displays their relatively straightforward shield designs by way of identification.

# THE DEVELOPMENT OF THE BLAZON

To describe a basic example of the creation of a blazon, the arms of the French family of d'Albret were originally simply "gules"—that is, plain—in this case, a red shield. However, in 1389 they were "augmented" with the arms of France, becoming *"Quarterly one and four Azure three fleurs de lis Or two and three Gules."* This is a classic description of a blazon, meaning that the shield was divided into four, quarters one and four were blue with three gold fleur de lys in each, while quarters two and three remained the original red color.

As heraldry developed, so did the sophistication of the coats of arms painted on shields. Accordingly, the language of the blazon also needed to develop, so that a clear message could be given to the artist as to exactly what to draw and paint onto the shield. The blazon needed to include all the details of tincture and number that an artist would need in order to reproduce the desired coat of arms accurately on the shield. The description always followed a set pattern according to a prescribed number of basic elements. These are outlined below but will be considered in detail later on, in Chapter 3 in the section dealing with shields, on pages 56 to 90.

## THE PRINCIPAL TERMS OF THE BLAZON

The following terms explain the main parts of any blazon, in the standard heraldic order:

THE FIELD This is the overall background of the shield, including any divisions—quarters, and such like—that might be applied upon it.

THE ORDINARIES These are the most simple "charges" or devices to be found on the heraldic shield. Also known as the "honorable ordinaries," they are geometric patterns laid over the field of the shield. There are many different ordinaries, with names such as the

"chief" (a bar across the top of the shield), the "fess" (a bar across the middle of the shield), and the "saltire" (a diagonal cross centered across the entire shield).

THE CHARGES These are the items actually painted onto the field once the field, divisions, and the ordinaries have been established. They are divided into "principal"—the main charges—and "lesser"—those charges of minor importance on the shield.

THE SUB-ORDINARIES These are the lesser geometric charges, with a host of exotic names varying from "bordure" (a painted border around the edge of the entire shield) to "lozenge" (a diamond shape painted in the middle of the field). These are normally deemed to be the less common of the geometric patterns found on shields of arms. However, like the ordinaries, their shapes were largely dictated by gradual developments in the construction of the medieval shield.

CHARGES ON THE SUB-ORDINARIES This term applies to all those lesser charges that might be painted onto the sub-ordinaries.

Beyond this basic classification of elements of the blazon, a more refined means of establishing the exact position on the shield that any charge might take evolved over a period of time. This involved the detailed naming of the different parts of and positions on the shield, starting with the "dexter and sinister"—the right and left sides of the shield— that are explained in detail on the following pages.

OPPOSITE: A 15th-century illustration of the Battle of Agincourt (1415). Only the more important figures in the painting are depicted wearing surcoats bearing their family arms. The lives of those French nobles thus identified would have been spared after the battle, and ransomed. In this respect, the accuracy of their coats of arms and the blazons that originally described them would have been of crucial importance.

# DEXTER AND SINISTER

ONE SOURCE OF ENDLESS CONFUSION IN THE STUDY OF HERALDRY IS THE QUESTION
OF RIGHT AND LEFT—THAT IS, WHICH SIDE OF THE COAT OF ARMS IS DEEMED THE
RIGHT SIDE AND WHICH THE LEFT. IN HERALDIC TERMINOLOGY THE RIGHT AND LEFT
SIDES OF A SHIELD ARE RESPECTIVELY KNOWN AS THE "DEXTER" AND THE "SINISTER."

## RIGHT AND LEFT

Right, called "dexter," and left, called "sinister,"
apply from the point of view of the person
carrying, or standing behind, the shield. So
"dexter" means *his* right as he stands opposite
you and you look at him. Similarly, "sinister"
means his left. The dexter, or right-hand side of
the bearer, is thought to be the most noble, and
most heraldic emblems are drawn facing that
way. It is only if they face in another direction
that any comment, or explanation, is required.

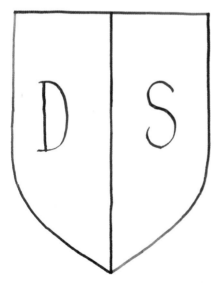

Medieval heraldic artists would often draw and
follow a basic shield outline with the letters
"D" and "S" arranged as shown to avoid any
confusion during their compositions.

The upper third portion of the field is called the
"chief"; the mid-point is the "fess-point"; and
the "nombril" is the point halfway between the
fess-point and the "base."

# RIGHT AND LEFT IN THE BLAZON

The principle of dexter and sinister is clearly seen in the Hungarian coat of arms below. The blazon describing the shield makes it quite clear how the various elements of the design work in relation to one another.

This is the coat of arms of the Hungarian village of Kőszárhegy in Fejér County. It displays a clear use of the principle of dexter and sinister and its detailed blazon—or heraldic description—is as follows:

*Triangular shield erect and collared. In the middle of the collar azure a heraldic rose is borne encoupé and argent. To the dexter and to the sinister from the charge of the rose a jug argent is borne on each side, with their loops turning outward. The two jugs are arranged symmetrically, although they are shaped differently. The one on the dexter side is round, while the one on the sinister side is octagonal. In the golden V-shaped field below the blue collar a vine stock is issuing from a regular mound vert. The vine stock is entwining a stick vert and it is holding a bunch of grapes and three leaves vert on the dexter and on the sinister side respectively.*

The interpretation of the settlement's coat of arms is as follows:

*Kőszárhegy is one of the younger settlements of Fejér County. The village separated from Szabadbattyán in 1931 and it received its present-day name in 1932. The "vine-hill of Szárhegy" was mentioned by contemporary documents as early as 1864. "Szárhegy" means a "bare hill" and there are several of this type all over Hungary. The first written mention of the word—in the form Zaarhegy—goes back to 1211. The regular-shaped green mound as well as the vine-stock are the charges which symbolize the 249 yard (228m) high local hill, after which the settlement got its name. The stylized rose is a reference to the archaeological site, where a world-famous silver treasure was found. The two silver jugs in the shield refer to the Sevso treasure.*

# THE USE OF COLORS

I F THERE IS ONE THING THAT MOST PEOPLE IMMEDIATELY ASSOCIATE WITH
HERALDRY, IT IS THE BOLD USE OF COLORS. THE BRIGHT REDS, GREENS, BLUES, AND
SO MANY OTHER TINCTURES EXCITE OUR VISUAL IMAGINATIONS POSSIBLY EVEN MORE
THAN THE FABULOUS ARRAY OF CHARGES THAT ADORNED MEDIEVAL COATS OF ARMS.

Even the most casual observer may be struck with delight by a bold and colorful heraldic display and it is important from the outset to discuss the heraldic colors and the ways in which they are used.

The student of heraldry will soon become aware that the basic colors used therein are in fact few; it is actually by skilful combinations of them that the most bold effects are produced. The colors, or tinctures, as they are properly called, must always be of the clearest and purest tone possible to give a bold, brilliant, and unambiguous effect. They were originally chosen so that the wearer would be readily identifiable at a distance, and in the "pell-mell" of battle, and their bold and striking combination is a vital part of the continuing tradition of heraldry.

The heraldic tinctures fall into three distinct groups: (1) those that represent metals; (2) those that represent colors; and perhaps strangely (3) those that represent furs.

## COLORS THAT REPRESENT METAL

The tincture white represents silver and is called "argent," abbreviated in blazons to "ar." The tincture yellow represents gold and is called "or."

It is quite proper to use silver or gold paint, but because of the difficulty of finding suitable pigments that will not blacken with age, it has become the custom to paint these tinctures with yellow and white. In very important documents it is customary to use gold or silver leaf on those parts that should be of these colors.

## TINCTURES THAT REPRESENT COLORS

These are listed below in the section on the importance of colors, each with its standard heraldic term and usual abbreviation. When a coat of arms is drawn in black and white, it is necessary to indicate what the tinctures are; a scheme of shading to use for each tincture has therefore also been developed. This is shown in a chart on page 52.

There was at one time a custom of describing the colors used by the planets and precious stones and metals. Because examples of this practice may still be found, they are set out in the table on page 53. The colors are red, blue, green, black, and purple.

There have been introduced in more recent times the following shades, or stains, as they are called—orange, blood red, mulberry purple, and sky blue. Their use is not widespread, although sky blue, as opposed to the true royal blue normally used, is increasingly being introduced, especially by people connected with aviation and space exploration.

## COLORS THAT REPRESENT FURS

Because of the importance of fur and its common use in contemporary dress, colors and patterns have been devised to represent fur in heraldry. The use of fur in a variety of forms is common in heraldry, though it does not necessarily indicate any special rank.
ERMINE The fur most commonly found is ermine, in its several forms. In northern climates the common stoat, a fierce, small, predatory

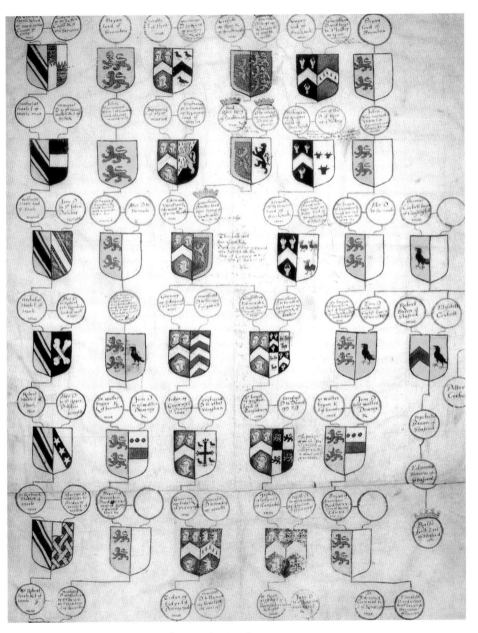

The 16th-century armorial family tree of Anne Hale. Note the use
of the colors yellow and white in place of gold and silver.

animal, normally colored a sandy chestnut, changes its coat to pure white in the winter, apart from the tip of the tail, which remains black. Ermine furs were highly prized and, because of their relative rarity and because of the large number of them needed, for example, to line a royal cloak, they were extremely expensive. They were sewn together, still with the tail attached, which hung loose. The heraldic representation of ermine is white, strewn with a regular black pattern representing the tails. A large number of designs have been recorded in heraldic representations of these tails.

Various combinations are also used, each with its own name:

ERMINE  White with black tails
ERMINOIS  Gold with black tails
ERMINES  Black with white tails
PEAN  Black with gold tails

VAIR (OR VAIRE, VAIRY, VERRE, VERREY, VERRY)  The next most common fur is vair, found in a variety of forms. It is always drawn as an alternating pattern of rounded or angular pieces of different colors. It is said by contemporary writers to represent the skins of the gray squirrel, sewn belly to back alternately, thus producing the white and blue pattern. Vair is always blue and white, unless other colors are specified, in which case the first color mentioned is always the piece in the top dexter corner. Vair is met in a variety of forms and these are shown opposite. A vair pattern of colors other than blue and white is always described as being "vairy of," whatever the colors specified. The most common forms of vair are vair, counter-vair, potent, counter-potent, vair ancient, and vary.

RIGHT: This chart shows the various combinations representing the tinctures of the two most common furs in heraldry, ermine and vair.

1 Ermine  2 Ermines  3 Erminois  4 Pean
5 Vair Ancient  6 Vair  7 Counter-Vair  8 Potent
9 Counter-Potent

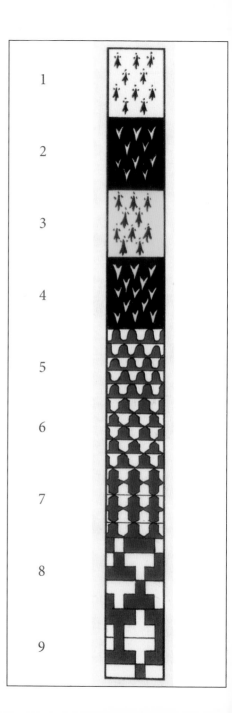

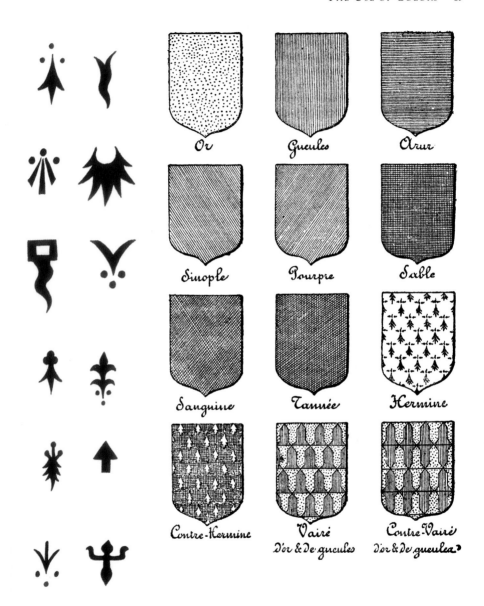

Or

Gueules

Azur

Sinople

Pourpre

Sable

Sanguine

Tannée

Hermine

Contre-Hermine

Vairé
D'or & De gueules

Contre-Vairé
D'or & De gueules

Many designs, of which a number are shown here, have been devised to represent ermine in heraldry. Each is a representation of the animal's tail.

This old engraved illustration shows a variety of enamel colors from heraldry, including variations of both ermine and vair. This illustration comes from the French Trousset encyclopedia (1886–1891).

# THE IMPORTANCE OF COLORS

WHILE IT WOULD APPEAR THAT BOLD COLORS WERE USED WITH ALACRITY BY THE HERALDIC ARTISTS, THERE WERE IN FACT A NUMBER OF STRINGENT RULES APPLIED TO THEIR USE. THESE WERE DEVISED IN THE INTERESTS OF VISUAL CLARITY AND ARTISTIC HARMONY, AND WOE BETIDE ANY ARTIST WHO DID NOT ABIDE BY THEM.

## THE RULES OF COLOR

To begin the blazoning of any coat of arms, a mention of color had to be made at the very outset. This was because the first word in the blazon—or description of the coat of arms—was "field," which primarily concerned the color of the background of the shield.

There are five main colors in heraldry (although this differs slightly in some countries)—red, blue, black, green, and purple. Some "stains," or mixed colors, were used in addition. Gold and silver would usually be depicted as yellow or white, although in very exclusive coats of arms actual gold or silver leaf would be used instead.

Given that the primary purpose of any coat of arms was for it to be clearly distinguishable on a shield in the heat of battle, it is not surprising that rules were soon laid down which were designed to ensure the ultimate visibility. These were as follows:

• Never place a metal on a metal, for example, a gold lion on a silver shield.

• Never place a color on another color, for example, a red lion on a blue shield.

• Always place a metal on a color or a color on a metal, for example, a gold lion on a red, blue, green, or black shield, or a red, blue, green, or a black lion on a silver or gold shield.

• A fur can take the place of a either a metal or a color.

All good rules exist to be broken, and there are plenty of examples of this in heraldry. However, these aberrations merely strengthened the need for the rules, which developed in the Middle Ages, and still endure today, long after heraldry's practical use has disappeared. That the rules have survived more or less intact until now must be some kind of proof of their worth.

## DIAPERING

When the Christian knights returned from the crusades they brought back with them fantastic brocades, woven materials, and silks that they had discovered in the sophisticated and civilized (compared to their own more robust environment) society that they encountered around the shores of the eastern Mediterranean. Ceremonial coats of arms and banners and flags were made of these new exotic materials.

Diapering was an attempt to repeat these fantastic patterns, as decorative treatment, on a painted shield, without diminishing the true color. It was usually carried out in a different shade of the same color or in painted gold. The patterns usually have an abstract swirl or leaf motif, though there are many examples in which geometric designs or very small, repeated heraldic devices were used.

Whenever a shield had a particularly large expanse of field, diapering could be used to stunning effect, adding textural interest to what might otherwise be a boring design. The main consideration was to ensure that the diapered pattern was not mistaken as part of the design.

Diapering (covering areas of flat color with a tracery design when depicting arms) is not considered a variation of the field; it is not specified in blazon, being a decision of the individual artist. This diapering is on the field of the shield of the Diocese of Worcester: argent, ten torteaux, four three two and one.

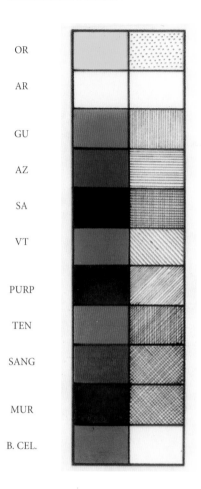

OR

AR

GU

AZ

SA

VT

PURP

TEN

SANG

MUR

B. CEL.

# HATCHING AND TRICKING

It was not always possible to use color in the depictions of coats of arms, so methods were devised to identify heraldic colors in black and white as well. These commonly involved two techniques that came to be known as "hatching" and "tricking," both of which are still commonly used in all forms of art to this day.

It was a 17th-century Italian Jesuit monk named Silvestro de Petra Sancta who came up with the system of showing colors represented by dots and lines that is universally known as hatching. This technique involved the application of lines of all angles and dispositions, sometimes criss-crossing one another, in order to denote specific colors. The designated hatching patterns are matched to their respective heraldic colors in the chart to the left.

Tricking was a variation on the theme, which involved the artist secreting tiny standard abbreviations for color names in parts of his black-and-white sketch. For example, any part of a design marked "gu" would be intended to be colored red and any marked "vt" would be green, and so on.

ABOVE: This chart shows the colors of heraldry, each accompanied by the abbreviation of its name (see the chart on the opposite page). Each color is also joined by the hatching pattern that was most commonly used with it in a design on a coat of arms.

RIGHT: This black-and-white heraldic design has been marked up with "tricking." The initials are interpreted as follows: arg = silver; gu = red; or = gold.

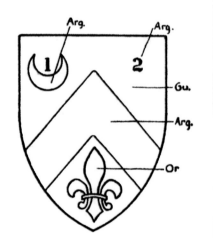

| | | | | | | |
|---|---|---|---|---|---|---|
| **THE COLORS OF HERALDRY** | | | | | | |
| **Color** | **Heraldic term** | **Abbreviation** | **Metal** | **Precious stone** | **Celestial body** | **Zodiac sign** |
| Gold | Or | or | Gold | Topaz | Sun | Leo |
| Silver | Argent | ar | Silver | Pearl | Moon | Cancer |
| Red | Gules | gu | Iron | Ruby | Mars | Aries |
| Blue | Azure | az or B | Tin | Sapphire | Jupiter | Taurus |
| Black | Sable | sa | Lead | Diamond | Saturn | Capricorn |
| Green | Vert or Sinople | vt | Copper | Emerald | Venus | Gemini |
| Purple | Purpure | purp | Quicksilver | Amethyst | Mercury | Sagittarius |
| Orange | Tenné | ten | | | | |
| Blood | Sanguine | sang | | | | |
| Mulberry | Murrey | mur | | | | |
| Sky blue | Bleu celeste | B. cel. | | | | |

# CHAPTER 3

# CONSTRUCTING A COAT OF ARMS

# THE SHIELD

AS WE HAVE SEEN EARLIER ON, HERALDIC DEVICES WERE ORIGINALLY USED TO IDENTIFY INDIVIDUALS IN BATTLE OR TO AUTHENTICATE DOCUMENTS AND INSTRUCTIONS BY WAY OF SEALS. ALTHOUGH THESE DEVICES WERE PAINTED ONTO A NUMBER OF DIFFERENT ITEMS AND ACCESSORIES, THE SHIELD WAS BY FAR THE MOST IMPORTANT OF THESE.

Heraldic devices were commonly applied to the shield, on to the coat of arms, on to the horse trappings, on flags, banners, and tents; essentially, they were used in every way possible to identify the wearer and owner. With the invention of guns in the 14th century, armor slowly began to fall into disuse, since it was no longer possible for a man both to be mobile and to wear armor sufficiently strong to stop bullet and ball. It therefore ceased to be difficult to identify men on the battlefield and heraldic insignia ceased to be used for this practical purpose by the 17th century. However, they have continued to be used as an artistic and traditional way in which to identify a person; and shields, though they no longer serve a protective function, have remained the chief vehicle upon which to display armorial insignia.

Armorial insignia are commonly depicted on other accessories and devices besides the shield. The whole assemblage is known as "the achievement," which is the correct term to describe the total collection of a person's heraldic accessories. They are also sometimes known as "appurtenances." Different countries and customs dictate that achievements contain different items. This chapter describes the parts of an achievement.

## THE SHIELD

The shield is the principal vehicle for the display of armorial insignia and is the only essential ingredient in an achievement of arms. The devices on the shield are the individual insignia—the armorial bearings—that distinguish one man from another. The shield is found in a variety of shapes and these are the result of different usages, fashions, and times. The principal shapes and styles are shown here.

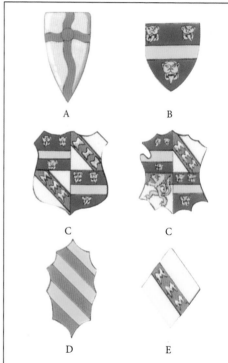

The principal shapes and styles of shields are as follows:
A the long shield; B the short or heater-shaped shield;
C the square-shaped shield (shown in two styles);
D the horsehead shield; and E the lozenge.

A ceremonial shield made in 15th-century Florence.
Note the diapering on the gold background.

The achievement of arms of a member of the Drury family, displayed
on a stained glass cartouche for hanging in a window.

**The long shield**, which gives the most protection, was used when men fought on foot. It afforded a protection against arrows, as well as in closer combat.

**The short or heater-shaped shield**, which was especially devised for use in tournaments, was strong enough to withstand a hit with a lance. Its shape provided the most protection and deflected the lance from the bearer. It was also called the "target," or "targ," after the point at which a knight aimed in a charge at a tournament.

**The square-shaped shield** became more popular when the custom developed of displaying more than one set of armorial bearings on one shield. This was because it offered a greater area of field than most other shield shapes, with better overall uniformity.

**The horsehead shield** is so called because its shape is thought to have developed from the armor plate used to protect the head and face of a knight's horse. It was quite often used by ecclesiastical dignitaries when the military-style shield was felt to be inappropriate.

**The lozenge and oval shield** Armigerous women customarily display their arms on an oval or a lozenge, since it has always been felt that it is inappropriate for a woman to display arms on a "military" shield.

**Ornamental cartouches and other shapes** Once the practical use of the shield disappeared, arms began to be displayed on all kinds of ornamental shapes and designs of a perplexing variety. Nowadays there has been something of a return to the beginnings of heraldry—to an earlier, simple style—and a simple shield is now fashionable once again. The square-shaped shield is used when several different armorial bearings are represented; the oval and the lozenge are still used to display women's heraldic devices. However, it should be made clear that the shape of the shield is not sacred; it can be changed, due consideration being given to style and period, to any shape that best suits the design of the armorial bearings that it displays or the article

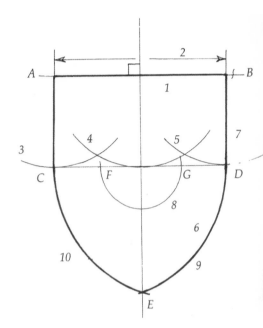

A simple method for constructing a quartered shield: draw two squares hanging from the line AB and from the points F and G respectively make the two arcs DE and CE. The proportions of the shield can be altered by altering the positions of F and G.

upon which it is placed. When it comes to shield design or a choice of shape, all that really matters is that the design conforms to heraldic ideals and is in good taste. Having said that, an appreciation of how the shield developed over hundreds of years and an understanding of why the various shapes evolved as they did will always positively inform a new personal design. An integral part of heraldry is respecting the rules and observances of the past.

OVERLEAF: A 13th-century illuminated manuscript depicting cavalry combat. The knights use their shields on their unprotected, usually the left-hand side, while wielding their swords with their right hand. Their shields bear their coat of arms identifying the owner in combat.

## DESCRIBING THE SHIELD

There are two ways, apart from painting or drawing a detailed picture of the coat of arms, by which the shield could be described. The first is the blazon (see page 40). All blazons follow a set pattern. Firstly, they describe the divisions of the field, if there are any, and the partition lines, if they are not straight. They consider next the main charge, then any secondary charges that may be placed either side of the main charge, and next any other charges that may be placed on the main charge.

The second is a method known as "the trick." This is a shorthand method of annotating a coat of arms, the sort of note that might be made to serve as a reminder of a coat of arms seen, for example, on a public building, in order to identify it later. This is the main use for the abbreviations in heraldry.

## THE FIELD

Before any design is placed on a shield, the shield is painted a color, which can be one of the metals, colors, or furs. As we have seen earlier in this book, there are examples of coats of arms that consisted of a plain tincture only. Bruget of Normandy bore a coat of arms and a shield "argent" (silver or white), the Duke of Brittany bore "ermine," and Berrington of Chester bore "azure." Notwithstanding all the things imaginable that might be placed on a blue shield, for example, it was soon necessary for differentiation to use two-colored shields, with one half red, say, and the other white.

## A FIELD SEMY, SEME, STREWN, OR POWDERED

Sometimes a field will be found strewn with many small charges and these are usually of a stated color. Some of them have their own special terms: "Semy de lis" or "semy of fleur de lis" means "representing the lily," while "crusiley" means that the field is strewn with little crosses. Other terms are "of the roundels," "loomme," "bezanty," "platy," "of the guttés," and "gutté d'or."

## THE DIVISIONS OF THE FIELD

The shield can be divided in a variety of ways and the form of the division and the colors to be used are always mentioned first in the blazon. Each different form of division of the field, has its own term, each of which is illustrated below. When describing a divided field, the color in the top dexter corner is always given first.

PER PALE

PER SALTIRE

# DIVISION OF THE FIELD

SALTIRE                    QUARTERLY

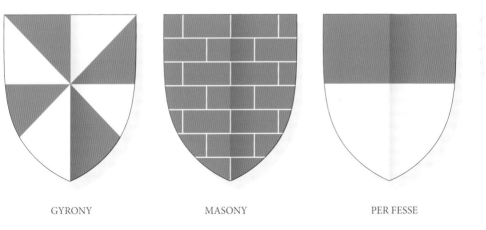

GYRONY                    MASONY                    PER FESSE

# DIVISION OF THE FIELD

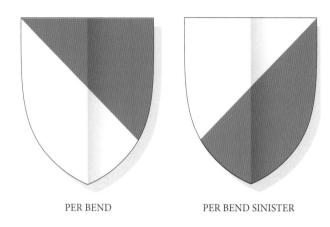

PER BEND                    PER BEND SINISTER

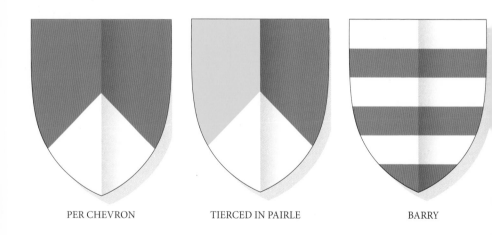

PER CHEVRON          TIERCED IN PAIRLE          BARRY

# DIVISION OF THE FIELD

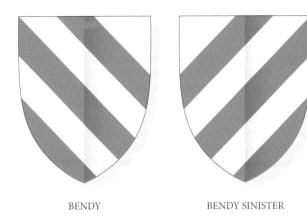

BENDY                    BENDY SINISTER

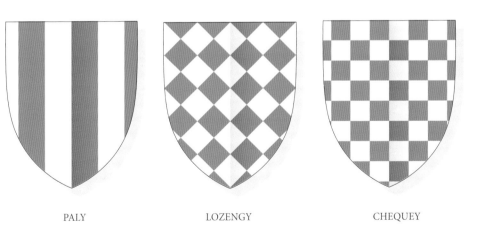

PALY                LOZENGY                CHEQUEY

## THE LINES OF PARTITION

In all the examples shown of divisions of the field on pages 62–5, the divisions are made with straight lines. They can, however, be made with a variety of zigzag or wavy lines, which are shown below. In a blazon the order of description is as follows: the division of the field (if any), the configuration of the line (if not straight), and the colors, the top dexter being first.

A FESS DANCY

A BEND WAVY

A FESSE EMBATTLED

A PALE INDENTED

A SALTIRE ENGRAILED

A FESSE WREATHY

# LINES OF PARTITION

DANCY

NEBULY

DOVETAILED

POTENTY

EMBATTLED

RAGULY

ENARCHED

RAYONNÉ

ENGRAILED

WAVY

FLORY/COUNTER-FLORY

WREATHY

INDENTED

URDY

Lines of partition can be drawn in many
different ways, as shown above.

## THE CHARGES

Any item placed upon the field of the shield is known as a "charge." If a shield has anything placed on it, it is said to be "charged" with that object. Similarly a lion with a rose on its shoulder is described as being "charged on the shoulder with a rose."

It has become the custom in an illustration of a coat of arms to show any charge placed upon the field as casting a shadow. As well as enhancing the artistic effect, the shadow shows that the item is not part of the field, but is charged upon it. The light is always shown as coming from the dexter top. The provision of a shadow is, however, by no means a rule and in small works it is frequently omitted for the sake of clarity. Charges of all kinds can themselves be charged in never-ending successions and combinations.

## THE ORDINARIES

This main group of charges consists of geometric shapes placed upon a shield, stripes in different combinations, and other shapes in addition. An ordinary usually takes up about one-third of the total area of the shield. It is important to remember that an ordinary is not a division of the field, but rather a charge placed upon it. All the main ordinaries are illustrated over the next few pages.

FESSE

BEND

# THE ORDINARIES

CHEVRON

CHIEF

CROSS

PALE

# THE ORDINARIES

PALL

BEND SINISTER

THREE BENDLETS
ENHANCED

# THE ORDINARIES

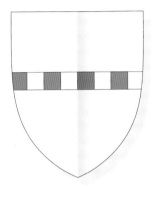

COMPONY

COUNTER COMPONY

CHEQUEY

## THE SUB-ORDINARIES

These are smaller geometric charges, less frequently used, but no less important. These too can soon be learned and, once remembered, are easily recognized.

TWO BARS

TWO BARS GEMEL

BARRULET

BATON

# THE SUB-ORDINARIES

TWO BENDLETS

THREE CHEVRONELS

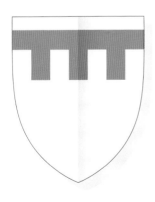

LABEL

BORDURE

# THE SUB-ORDINARIES

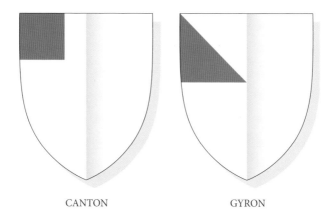

CANTON                    GYRON

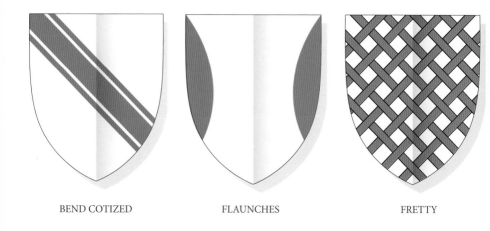

BEND COTIZED          FLAUNCHES          FRETTY

# THE SUB-ORDINARIES

CROSS FIMBRIATED                    FRET

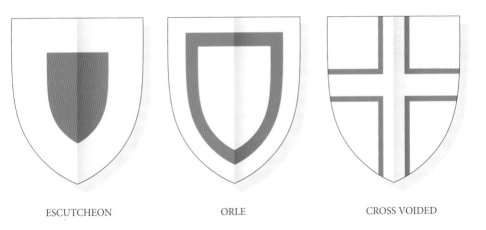

ESCUTCHEON              ORLE              CROSS VOIDED

## THE ROUNDELS AND GUTTÉ

The "roundels" appear as different colored circles, each with their own name. A gold roundel is a "bezant;" a silver roundel is called a "plate;" red, a "torteau;" bloodred, a "guze;" blue, a "hurt;" green, a "pomme;" black, a "pellate;" "ogress," or "gunstone;" purple a "golpe;" orange, an "orange;" and when barry, wavy, argent or azure, a "fountain."

"Gutte" (or "gutty," "gouty") means "strewn with droplets." Like the roundels, they have a different name for each color. "Gutté d'or" describes a field or charge strewn with gold drops; "gutté d'eau," silver drops; "gutté de sang," red drops; "gutté de larmes," blue drops; "gutté de poix," black drops; and "gutté d'huile" (or more rarely, "d'olive"), green drops.

COMBINATIONS Combinations of these groups are frequently seen.
COUNTERCHANGING This feature is quite often encountered, in which a charge is placed over a divided field and the colors reversed. Some exciting and exotic effects could be produced by this method.
OTHER CHARGES Any object may be placed upon a shield either on its own or in combination with the ordinaries, sub-ordinaries, or other unrelated objects. Charges may be of any color, including their own natural color, and they may be countercharged with the field or the ordinaries, sub-ordinaries, or be themselves charges with other charges. The variety is endless, and needed to be, to ensure that each coat of arms was unique. The only limitations were those imposed by good taste and the rule of tincture concerning the use of color, metal, and fur.
CANTING ARMS Many charges that appeared on coats of arms often related to the name of the bearer of those arms. This was a common practice in medieval and later heraldry but, unfortunately, with the gradual change of language over the centuries, the meaning of the allusion has often been lost.

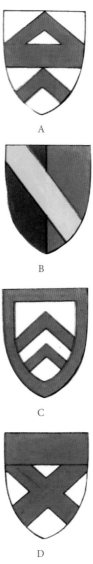

Four combinations of ordinaries and sub-ordinaries are illustrated above, with the name of the arms bearer given in brackets: A Argent a fesse between two chevrons gules (Fitzwalter); B Per pale azure and gules overall a bend or (Langton); C Argent two chevrons with a bordure gules (Albini); D Argent a saltire and chief gules (Bruce).

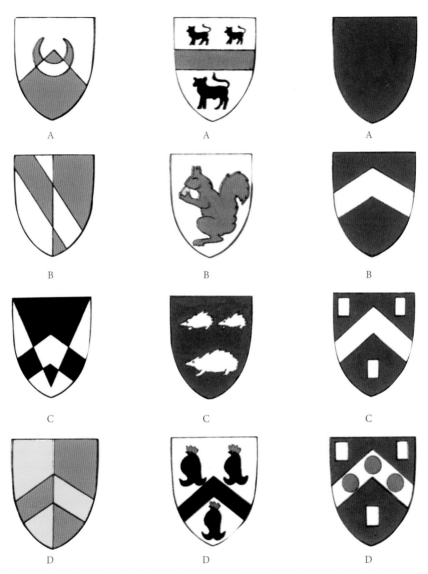

A

A

A

B

B

B

C

C

C

D

D

D

LEFT: Four examples of counterchanging: A per chevron argent and gules overall a crescent counterchanged (Barker) B per pale argent and gules overall a bend counterchanged (Chaucer) C argent a pile and a chevron countercharged, and D per pale or and gules a chevron counterchanged (Chambers). CENTER: Four examples of canting arms: A argent between three calves sable a fesse gules (Calverly); B argent a squirrel gules eating a gold nut (Squires); C azure three hedgehogs argent (Harris); and D argent between three moorcocks a chevron sable (Moore). RIGHT: A shield has four main elements to be described in a blazon: A the color of the shield (azure); B the main charges (on a chevron); C the secondary charges (between three billets argent); and D any additional charges (three torteaux).

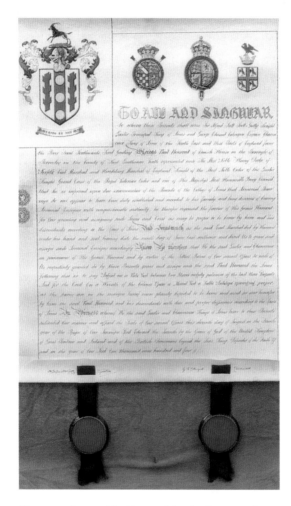

The grant of arms of the Henwood family of Kent. Such
documents conferring arms are issued in the same form by
the heralds of England and Scotland to the present day.

An achievement of arms of one of the many armigerous Smith families, showing argent on a fess nebuly counter-nebuly sable three rabbits' heads erased argent, in the second and third quarters.

# THE HELMET

Medieval combat was fierce, intensely violent and dangerous, so adequate protection for warriors' heads was vital. The earliest helmets were basic and uncomplicated, but as the sophistication of weapons and fighting methods increased, so the quality and range of helmets developed exponentially.

In the days of hand-to-hand warfare, adequate protection for the head was provided by a simple iron cap or basinet, which was sufficient to protect the wearer from sword blows. Later a noseplate and cheek plates were added. When cavalry was introduced the helmet had to be much stronger and so the helmet which closed with a visor and which had a plate around the neck—a gorget— was introduced. Helmets with bars and grids across the face were also introduced.

Ceremonial helmets, usually of the type with bars, were made of softened leather and were richly decorated. They were used as vehicles to display the crest, especially in countries where whole families display the same armorial bearings on the shield and identify the individual only by a different crest.

In some countries it is the custom to use different types and posture of helmet, or "helm," as it is more usually called, to differentiate men according to this social rank. This, however, is only a custom, not a rule, and it is often broken.

## THE POT HELM
This, the oldest type of helm, was worn over the top of the small basinet and chain-mail gorget. Its use in heraldry is limited to gentlemen in Scotland and some families of ancient lineage, in Germany and Denmark.

## THE TILTING HELM
This helm was used by gentlemen and esquires in England, the Scandinavian countries, Germany, and Poland, and (though less

commonly), by persons of all ranks throughout Europe. Some members of the German, Austrian, Hungarian, and Polish nobility have used it to show that their armorial bearings are of more ancient lineage than those depicted by "newer men" on the more modern barred helm. It is also used in Italian heraldry for non-titled ranks. Civic and corporate armorial bearings in England usually use this type of helm.

It is common in heraldry for helmets to be featured in coats of arms, as here, in which a highly decorated helm with open visor sits atop an heraldic shield.

A modern re-creation of a crusading Knight Templar's helmet, of the pot helm variety.

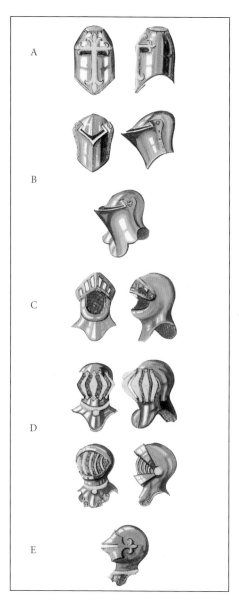

A

B

C

D

E

## THE HELM WITH OPEN VISOR AND NO BARS

This type is used, usually facing the front, by British knights and baronets (hereditary knights) and Russian Leibkanpanez.

## THE BARRED HELM

This helm, found in a variety of forms and styles, is used all over Europe, usually to denote titled rank—though in Belgium, the Netherlands, and Spain it is used by untitled ranks as well. The posture of the helm varies from country to country, and alterations in the number of bars and the artistic treatment are then used to signify distinctions of rank. An English peer of whatever rank, for example, uses a five-barred helm facing to the left (as you look at it). On the continent, this helm, whether facing the front or either side, is used by all ranks. In Italy and Spain the posture, the number of bars, and the amount of gold used demonstrate the rank of the bearer. In Denmark and the Netherlands a silver helm is used for non-titled persons, gold for peers.

## THE ARMET

This helm, with the visor open or closed and with or without bars, is used in Italian and Spanish heraldry and, to a lesser extent, in France. Its style is quite different from that of the other helms used in European heraldry, so that its use in an achievement may give a good clue to the bearer's origins. All the European sovereigns have used gold helms, facing the front and topped by a royal crown. In England the royal helm shows eight bars; others show a gold helm with the visor open.

   Although the conventions that govern the use of helms are not rules (despite attempts to standardize the use of helms to indicate the rank of the wearer), there are discernible national styles that should help students to discover the origin and rank of the wearer. But the helm alone is never conclusive evidence; it should be considered with caution and assessed in the context of the style of the other items of the achievement.

Various types of helmets are represented here: A the pot helm; B the tilting helm; C the helm with open visor and no bars; D the barred helm; E the armet.

In keeping with the diversity of heraldic design, in medieval times the styles of both helmets and accompanying armor were spectacularly numerous and multifarious. This unusual barred helmet sits above a sleeveless metal tunic.

# THE CREST

SECOND ONLY TO THE SHIELD, THE CREST IS A HIGHLY IMPORTANT CONSTITUENT PART OF ANY ACHIEVEMENT OF ARMS. IT IS THE THREE-DIMENSIONAL OBJECT THAT ADORNS THE TOP OF A HELMET. ALTHOUGH FORMERLY INTRODUCED AS TRUE HERALDIC ARMS IN THE MIDDLE AGES, CRESTS FEATURED ON HELMETS FOR CENTURIES BEFORE.

It can be seen from examining any achievement of arms showing a helmet that it is very unusual for the helmet to have nothing placed upon it. Usually a helmet bears a crest. The crest is a product of the tournament, and because of the importance of pageantry and display in a tournament, the crest, which was proudly fixed atop the helm, became increasingly complicated and large. Every kind of emblem—carved of wood or made of leather and stiffened canvas and richly painted and gilded—was devised, and the devices chosen were representations of every kind of thing imaginable. Sometimes they repeated the devices on the armorial bearings, or a part of them; often they were any other thing, real or imaginary, that could be contrived to sit securely atop the helm.

In England nowadays the practice is for all members of a family to exhibit the same crest, but there are several instances of unrelated families displaying similar crests, so that the crest is not a reliable emblem of identification. When family ties and tradition are felt to be important, the crest is displayed on its own, especially on items such as rings, silver, china, and glass, that are likely to be handed down from one generation to the next.

On the Continent, where families display the same armorial bearings, each member sports a different crest, by which he may be recognized. It is therefore a very personal emblem. It was often the practice, before a tournament, for helmets, with their crests, to be displayed for inspection, especially by ladies of the court. If a lady espied the crest of someone who had in

any way wronged any of her number, she would touch the helm and it would be thrown to the floor by a herald. The owner was not then able to take part in the tournament and there was nothing for it but for him to pick up his helm and slink off in disgrace.

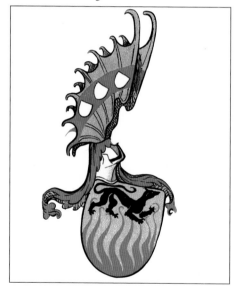

ABOVE: A decorated shield and helm in the traditional medieval style utilizing animal and other symbols in the creation of a chivalric identity.

OPPOSITE: A chair-back in the House of Lords, worked in tapestry representing the Royal Arms of England. The crest is a lion *statant* (standing), *guardant* (front-facing), above a royal crown on a gold helm with seven bars.

A selection of different medieval helm crests and decorations.

A traditional shield, helm, and crest featuring a double-headed Byzantine eagle.

# CHAPEAUX AND CREST CORONETS

CHAPEAUX AND CREST CORONETS WERE HIGHLY COLORFUL AND DECORATIVE HELMET EMBELLISHMENTS THAT BECAME AN IMPORTANT PART OF TOURNAMENT RITUAL IN EUROPE IN THE LATER MIDDLE AGES. ALTHOUGH THEY WERE OFTEN VERY LARGE AND CUMBERSOME, THESE ITEMS WERE FIXED TO KNIGHTS' HELMETS AS A MATTER OF COURSE.

In the later Middle Ages, it became necessary to modify the rules of the tournament—due to the fact that so many good men were being killed. One of the new practices adopted was to supply each competing knight with a club, so that opponents could strike at one another, while mounted on their horses, until the crest of one or the other had been knocked to the ground, and the loser had been metaphorically toppled into the dust. The crest was secured to the top of the helm as securely as possible and the crude fixings that were used were in turn covered by the following three items.

## THE TORSE OR WREATH
This is always represented by different colored materials, twisted together and tied around the helm to cover the gap between the crest and helm. The torse is thought to have originated from the tournament, when a knight would collect from the crowd a "favor" from his most esteemed lady to show that he fought for her honor and as her champion. He would tie the item around his helm. In Great Britain the torse or wreath now consists of six twists of alternating color, always with a metal color (silver or gold) coming first. On the Continent it is often made up of five or seven segments instead, so that a symmetrical design is produced. In Italy a slim torse of ten or twelve sections is used. In Spain, where crests are not used, untitled persons use a plume of ostrich feathers, which are held in place by a torse placed vertically over the crown of the helm. The torse is also used in France, in both forms, and in Holland and Germany.

## THE CHAPEAU
In Great Britain, helms are sometimes seen with the crest standing on what appears to be a red cap with a turned-up ermine lining, which is placed over the top of the helm, with no torse. This is a symbol of royal privilege and is seldom encountered. In Scotland, hereditary barons use a blue chapeau as an emblem of their rank.

## THE CREST CORONET
Often found atop a helmet is a crest coronet, in place of the torse, out of which issues the crest. This simple coronet is found throughout Europe and the crest coronet should not be confused with a coronet of rank, which is displayed by peers, princes, and sovereigns (see pages 96–7). It has been used as a decorative feature, perhaps to invest the wearer with a dignity that he might otherwise not have. It should be pointed out that Spain and Italy use coronets of rank with no crest atop the helm, although in Italy the coronet always sits on a narrow torse. Italy, like Spain, does not use crests. Helms with coronets of rank are found in Russian, Polish, Hungarian, and Scandinavian heraldry. Apart from their decorative function, the torse, the wreath, and the crest coronet are all designed to hold the mantling in place on the helm.

Napoleon tried to sweep away all French heraldry associated with royalty and introduced a new system. In the place of helmets and crests a series of black caps, known as Napoleonic caps, each with different plumes and colored headbands, was introduced to indicate rank.

The crest coronet.

The torse or wreath.

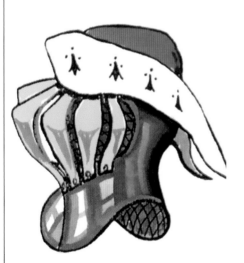

The chapeau.

The torse or wreath.

The torse or wreath.

The Spanish torse.

The original royal crest as introduced by Edward III, borne
upon a chapeau and with a red mantling lined in ermine.
The steel helm has gold embellishments.

# MANTLING OR LAMBREQUIN

THE COMPLETE HERALDIC ACHIEVEMENT OF ARMS IS A THOROUGHLY GRAND AFFAIR
THAT CONSISTS OF SEVERAL DIFFERENT COMPONENT PARTS. AFTER THE SHIELD, THE
HELMET, AND THE CREST COMES THE MANTLING—A LOOSE PIECE OF CLOTH THAT HANGS
DOWN FROM THE TOP OF THE HELMET, SEEN IN A VARIETY OF COLORS AND DESIGNS.

When the crusaders went to free the Holy Land, fitted out with all the extensive weaponry, armor, and accoutrements of war of medieval knights, they soon discovered that they were ill equipped to fight in a hot, dusty, and arid climate. They rapidly adopted the native practice of wearing a small cloak or cloth fastened to the top of the helm to keep the sun off their backs. That covering became known as the "mantling."

It became fashionable for medieval knights to have their mantling slashed to pieces, so as to show that they had been in many fierce battles. This ostentatious custom accounts for the fantastic designs and shapes of mantling that may be encountered in heraldic design, from the simple, restrained kerchief hanging at the back of the helm (usually seen with the early pot helm designs of helmet) to the wildly extravagant swirls and masses that have become so exaggerated that they have earned the description "mass of seaweed."

It is usual for the mantling to be of two colors, the principal metal color of the armorial bearings on the inside and on the outside the principal color. In describing mantling, the outside color is always mentioned first, and then the inside, describing the latter as "turned or doubled," whichever it may be. It is not unusual to find mantling of two or more outside colors, nor to find them turned, doubled, or lined with a fur, or with metals of different colors. You may find the outside strewn with devices, sometimes echoing those displayed on the shield, or find them

covered with badges. Sometimes, when the crest is an animal or person, the mantling is a continuation of the skin of the animal or the vesture of the person.

An ancient mantling design, in the form of a swan with a long flowing tail, attached to the oldest and most basic type of helmet, the pot helm.

The arms of the Aragonese monarchs of the 16th to 19th centuries featured some quite dramatic mantling or lambrequin in azure and gules.

Another design of mantling, this one from the later Middle Ages. This green and yellow embellishment is styled with what is known as "fanciful elaboration."

This more modern design is simpler, but the mantling is larger in relation to the other elements of the achievement.

Mantling could be as colorful and elaborate as a knight could imagine or afford.
There was no limit to the range of designs that were seen on the medieval battlefield.

# CORONETS, INSIGNIA, AND MEDALS

I N ALL COUNTRIES THAT HAVE ADOPTED HERALDRY, IT IS POSSIBLE TO FIND SYSTEMS WITHIN THE HERALDIC CODE THAT ARE DESIGNED EXCLUSIVELY TO DENOTE RANK AND STATUS. THE MOST COMMONLY DEPLOYED DEVICES IN THIS BRANCH OF HERALDRY ARE MADE UP OF A WIDE VARIETY OF CORONETS, INSIGNIA, AND MEDALS.

## THE USE OF MORE THAN ONE HELM AND CREST

When different armorial achievements become invested in one person, it is quite common to find more than one helm and crest used on an achievement; in German heraldry as many as twelve may be used. In Great Britain, where it is unusual to find more than three, it is the practice to place all the helms facing the dexter. On the Continent they are placed to respect each other, the most important on the dexter side, or in the middle if there are more than two.

## CORONETS OF RANK

In the achievements of peers, it is common to find displayed between the shield and the helms the coronet of rank. This is common practice in most European countries, except Spain, Portugal, and Italy, where no crest is used and the coronet is placed on the helm. It is also common for peers simply to display a shield showing their armorial devices and their coronets of rank. It is important not to confuse coronets of rank with crest coronets or heraldic crowns, which are discussed on pages 88–91.

Prince

Marquis

Duke

Viscount

Earl

Baron

Each rank of the English nobility has its own coronet, as illustrated here.

The three coats of arms shown here are: (*top left*) the arms of Baron Manvers; (*top right*) the arms of the
Duke of Argyll (showing the emblem of the Hereditary Grand Master of the Household and Hereditary
Justice-General of Scotland); and (*bottom*) the arms of the Earl Marshal of England (showing the batons of
office and the blue ribbon of the Garter).

The armorial bearings of Sir Ronald Gardner-Thorpe show the circlet of a Knight of the British Empire, with the badge of the order on the ribbons below, and the Cross of the Order of the Knights of St. John.

## INSIGNIA OF OFFICE

It is quite common for insignia denoting some office held by the bearer of the achievement —such as the two crossed batons of the Earl Marshal of England—to be placed behind the shield.

## THE CHAINS, MEDALS, AND CROSSES OF ORDERS OF CHIVALRY

It is not uncommon to find placed behind the shield a cross of an order of chivalry, which denotes that the bearer is a knight commander of the relevant order. Ribands of chivalric orders of knighthood, with the motto of the order on them, are also found encircling shields. Knights of the order may encircle their riband with the chain collar of the order. Badges or decorations, of an order, in the lesser ranks, may be hung below the shield, shown suspended from ribands.

BELOW: This cross represents the Order of the Crown of Prussia from the 19th century and bears the legend "Gott mit uns"—God with us.

# THE ROLE OF SUPPORTERS

ON MANY ACHIEVEMENTS OF ARMS THE SHIELD AND THE HELM SOMETIMES APPEAR AS IF THEY ARE BEING HELD UP BY TWO ANIMALS OR OTHER BEINGS, ACTING AS SUPPORTERS. THIS PRACTICE HAS BEEN UNDERTAKEN SINCE THE EARLIEST DAYS OF HERALDRY AND REMAINS AN IMPORTANT ASPECT OF ITS TRADITIONS TO THIS DAY.

The inclusion of supporters in heraldic achievements of arms is thought to have been begun by seal engravers, who sought to fill in the space between the side of the engraved shield and the round edge of the seal with images of mythical beasts such as small dragons. The practice of using supporters probably became widespread with the rise of the tournament, at which knights employed their pages to parade around the arena, carrying their masters' shields and dressed in fantastic costumes, to the delight of the crowd. At these events, supporters in the form of monsters were particularly popular, with the costumed servants looking as ferocious as possible, while pretending to be giants or wild men of the woods.

## THE RULES THAT DEFINE SUPPORTERS

Supporters may take any form, from animals or humans to mythical or celestial beings. It is more usual to find two supporters, one on each side, although frequently only one is used. The use of supporters varies greatly from country to country and care should be taken not to confuse supporters that are properly part of the achievement of arms with those that have been added purely for artistic effect.

In Great Britain, supporters may be granted by the appropriate authority as part of the achievement of arms and handed down from father to son. They may be used by peers, senior ranks of some civic authorities, and corporate bodies. The same is true in Scotland, where the controlled use of supporters is also

extended to some barons and clan chiefs. In the Netherlands there are no restrictions on their use. In Germany and Austria they are used only by the higher ranks of the peerage; but there is no definite rule and peers quite often do not use them. It is common for the national arms of this area, and those of its sovereigns and princes, to use one supporter—the eagle—in its many different forms, with the shield displayed on the breast. Italy, Spain, and Portugal generally do not use supporters. In Belgium their use is generally confined to the nobility and to some civic authorities.

Supporters can be two identical beings or two that are completely dissimilar. They may be carrying any kind of weapon or banner or any other object appropriate to the bearer. Flying birds are sometimes used, or two ships. It is perfectly permissible to show armorial bearings that should have supporters without them; for although they may form part of a grant of armorial bearings they are, like everything else but the shield, not essential elements of an achievement of arms.

## THE MANTEAU OR ROBE OF ESTATE AND PAVILION

Princes, the higher representatives of the nobility, and certain high officials of secular bodies or the church display their entire achievements of arms upon a representation of a draped cloak, usually with a color on the outside and one of the furs within. There are many varieties of this custom, though it is not practiced in Great Britain.

An achievement of arms with griffin supporters.

## SUPPORTERS AS PROPAGANDA

A large part of heraldry is the promotion of social status and the ancestry by which it is so often conferred. As most members of the nobility of Europe like to trace their ancestral line back to a warrior forebear, it is therefore not surprising to find military figures supporting the shields of many titled families.

Soldiers are often depicted as supporters, not only to commemorate the military deeds of ancestors but also to celebrate the exploits of a living family member in a particular battle or campaign. If an event is significant enough—particularly one that is military in nature—it will soon be incorporated in an achievement of arms. Supporters of this kind are especially popular in British and Russian heraldry and can also been seen on the shields of various Hungarian courts, in which hussars are often given a starring role. Right across Europe, depictions of armored knights were very popular in the 18th and early 19th centuries.

The achievement of arms of the Borough of Beccles follows the usual practice of including two supporters.

A lone griffin supports this shield bearing the coat of arms of the City of London.

# TYPES OF SUPPORTERS

IN HERALDIC ART, IT IS THE DEPICTION OF SUPPORTERS THAT PROBABLY OFFERS THE MOST SCOPE FOR THE IMAGINATION OF THE DESIGNERS BEHIND CLASSIC ACHIEVEMENTS OF ARMS. ALTHOUGH IMAGES OF SUPPORTERS MUST CONFORM TO CORRECT HERALDIC POSTURE AND TINCTURE, THERE IS MUCH ROOM FOR ARTISTIC LICENCE.

Designs involving supporters offer the artist great flexibility with regard to style and in the design of the whole achievement, allowing a balanced composition to be created that is both fitting for the shape of the space available and which reflects the style of the time in which it was rendered.

Heraldic supporters are interesting primarily because of the amazing variety of creature that is employed. Every kind of mythical and real creature is brought into use and can be found bearing their master's arms with pride across the pages of history. Lord Twining uses a crested crane and a giraffe. Cobbold has two yellow labradors. Freyberg two salamanders proper (a salamander proper is depicted bright red and in flames). These were no doubt used as an allusion to the name. The City of Inverness uses an elephant and camel and Australia uses a kangaroo and an emu.

## AN ARRAY OF ANIMALS AND MYTHICAL BEASTS

There are numerous examples of lions, stags, hounds of many different kinds, and horses, some of which are mounted. Lord Birdwood employs dexter a Sergeant of the XII Bengal Lancers mounted on a bay horse and sinister a Sikh Daffador of XI Bengal Lancers mounted on a chestnut horse, both habited and accoutred proper. Bulls, bears, wolves, and boars are commonly found, as are even the tiny ermine and its larger cousin the otter.

The mythical creatures appear in equal array. Dragons and griffins are commonly used

and so is the wyvern. Lord Arbuthnot uses two wyverns, vert, their tails nowed (knotted together) vomiting flames proper. Heraldic panthers, antelopes, yale, and tigers appear. (For information about all these creatures, see the section on mythical creatures in Chapter 4, pages 164–167).

## HUMAN BEINGS AS HERALDIC SUPPORTERS

Human beings are used in every variety. Serving officers tend to show supporters of the units with which they served. Lord Baden Powell had an officer of the 13th/18th Hussars, his sword drawn over his shoulder and a boy scout holding a staff proper, representing the regiment with which he served and the world famous youth movement that he founded. Admiral Lord Fisher uses on either side a sailor of the Royal Navy supporting an anchor, cabled all proper. The Worshipful Company of Farmers bears on either side a farmworker proper. Both these achievements used supports dressed as of the time when they were granted. Uniform and dress have changed over the years. A farmworker drawn now might more properly be depicted in wellington boots, a green overall, rubber gloves, and a sprayhood! It is important for the heraldic artist to bear these differences in mind and as far as possible illustrate such things in the costume of the period of the original grant, if this can be ascertained.

It is quite common to find clerics of different denominations and sometimes saints. Wild men or savages are fairly commonly employed,

The armorial bearings of the Worshipful Company of Farmworkers.

The armorial bearings of the Worshipful Company of Fishmongers.

depicted as naked, with a wreath of leaves about the loin and head and usually wielding a large club. Women also appear, as serving members of nursing or military units, or simply as maidens, more or less dressed. The Worshipful Company of Needlemakers use a representation of Adam and Eve wreathed about the waist with fig leaves, sewn proper. The Worshipful Company of Glaziers has on either side a boy proper holding in the exterior hand a torch or, inflamed proper. These boys are always drawn naked, as no mention is made of their vesture.

## ANGELS, HARPIES, MERMAIDS, MERMEN, AND TRITONS

Of the human monsters and mythical beings, angels appear quite often. An angel is supposed to be shown sexless and it is not really correct to draw it as a nubile young female, as is sometimes seen. They are usually shown in a long straight gown, with just feet and hands visible, long fair hair, and wings. Those fearful creatures, the harpies, are used as supporters and so too are mermaids, mermen, or tritons. The Worshipful Company of Fishmongers (see the illustration on the opposite page) bears dexter a merman holding in his right hand a falchion (a type of sea axe) sinister a mermaid holding in her left hand a mirror, all proper. Mermaids are very vain and beautiful beings and are shown with a mirror and usually a comb. The late Welsh actor, comedian, and singer Sir Harry Secombe had as a charge a mermaid combing her hair (sea comb) and a motto in English which said "Go on"—one of his comedic catchphrases. Such elegant and simple blazonry embodies the spirit and imagination that is the very essence of heraldry.

## BIRDS AS SUPPORTERS

Birds too play an important part in this area of heraldry, and eagles and falcons abound as supporters. The Spectacle Makers have two falcons (keen sight). The Emperors of the Holy Roman Empire used one double-headed eagle, displayed (to show dominion over East

A stone carving by S. & J. Winter illustrates the use of a single supporter in heraldry—in this case, a horse.

This is a modern take on a classic heraldic design featuring a double-headed Byzantine eagle as the supporter of a shield.

Fish of all descriptions crop up remarkably frequently in heraldic design, sometimes as supporters in the most unlikely positions and postures.

and West) and charged their arms upon its breast. As with animals, all kinds of birds are used as supporters in heraldry. Ostriches, lyre-birds, parrots, albatrosses, doves, and condors—all these have featured in designs, as have even two mallards, larks, and goldfinches. The Scrivener's Company have two secretary birds. Lord Brabazon bears so elegantly on either side, supporting the shield in its beak, a gull volant (flying) over water, proper.

## FISH AS SUPPORTERS

Even fish are enrolled in this noble task. Lord Temnart bears two dolphins proper and the City of Glasgow bears on either side a salmon haurient, bearing in its mouth a ring or, enjewled gules. This is in honour of the legend of St. Kentirgern who came there and worked many miracles, one of which was to restore Queen Rederech's lost ring to her with the aid of a salmon.

## INANIMATE OBJECTS

As well as all the beings of creation and of myth and imagination, some inanimate objects have been employed. The City of Southampton uses on either side on the quarter-deck of a two-masted sailing vessel on the sea, proper, a lion rampant or. Lord Boyd Orr uses two wheat sheaves.

# THE GRIFFIN AS HERALDIC SUPPORTER

### MALE GRIFFIN

The male griffin is always depicted with tusks on its lower beak and spines emanating from its back.

### FEMALE GRIFFIN

The female griffin is always drawn with wings.

The griffin is the king of all the creatures. Whilst the lion is the king of the beasts and the eagle is the king of the birds, the griffin that bears a combination of the best attributes of both these magnificent creatures, like a good claret, is better than the sum of its constituent parts. Its amalgamation gains in courage and boldness. Its fierceness and strength are increased. It is used to denote strength and military courage and leadership. It is composed of the head, neck, and fore feet of an eagle, with the body, back legs, and tail of a lion.

# THE COMPARTMENT

ALTHOUGH THERE ARE NO HARD-AND-FAST RULES ON THE SUBJECT IN HERALDIC DESIGN, IT IS GENERALLY FELT THAT SUPPORTERS OF ACHIEVEMENTS OF ARMS SHOULD HAVE SOMETHING TO STAND UPON. THIS CAN BE ANYTHING FROM SOLID GROUND TO THE RIBAND OF A MOTTO, AND IS GENERICALLY KNOWN AS THE "COMPARTMENT."

Although most heraldic supporters are depicted standing upon some item or another, there are actually plenty of examples of achievements of arms in which supporters are literally left hanging in the air, without a compartment. The compartment may consist of almost anything. It may represent the ground beneath your feet—often strewn with herbage or flowers, or badges—water, or simply ornamental scroll work. An inscribed motto riband is also sometimes used, although examples of this are more rare.

## EARLY USE OF THE COMPARTMENT

When compartments first came to be designed in heraldry, during the early Middle Ages, they were nearly always made as a representation of solid ground. Nobody knows why flimsy scrolls and more formal platforms enjoyed popularity in later decades, but this might be because very often the compartment was not included in the blazon. This was certainly the case whenever grassy mounds were depicted, in which case the heraldic artist had a lot more scope for his imagination. Today, the compartment has become an official part of the blazon in heraldry and stricter rules about the way they are depicted now apply.

## RENAISSANCE COMPARTMENTS

The compartment enjoyed its greatest popularity during the Renaissance, when heraldic artists expressed the aesthetic motivation of the period by depicting the arms in elaborate frameworks. In many of these later designs the supporters were placed on grandiose pedestals embellished with classical motifs, masks, foliage, and strapwork. Just as these representations of the compartment were typical of the artistic flair of the Renaissance, so later artistic periods lent their own styles and characteristics to shield supporters and compartments alike.

## MODERN COMPARTMENTS

The compartment is favored by many civic and academic authorities applying for arms these days, possibly because it seems to confer greater importance to many heraldic designs.

The armorial bearings of the Chelmsford Borough Council, engraved by Stefan Oliver, have an unusual compartment, consisting of a bridge over water, retained by a motto riband.

The arms of the Republic of South Africa feature a classic grassy mound as the compartment. The official blazon for this coat of arms is as follows: quarterly per fess wavy: I, gules, a female figure representing Hope, resting the dexter arm upon a rock, and supporting with the sinister an anchor argent; II, or, two black wildebeest in full course at random, both proper; III, or, upon an island an orange tree vert fructed proper; IV, vert, a trek wagon argent.

# MOTTOES

MANY COATS OF ARMS INCLUDE A SINGLE WORD OR SHORT SENTENCE KNOWN IN HERALDRY AS THE "MOTTO." THE POSITIONING OF THESE IS CONSIDERABLY MORE RANDOM THAN FOR OTHER ELEMENTS OF THE ACHIEVEMENT OF ARMS AND VARIES FROM COUNTRY TO COUNTRY, AS DOES THE IMPORTANCE OF THE MOTTO.

Mottoes are found in achievements of arms all over the world, but they are a relatively recent innovation in heraldry and matter a great deal more in some places than others. In Scotland, for example, they are regarded as an essential ingredient of any coat of arms and are placed on a riband above the helm. Contrarily, in England, as in the rest of Europe, they are not regarded as a formal part of the achievement, but they may, if desired, be placed below the shield.

The riband containing the motto is usually drawn as ornately as the style and period allow and is usually shown white outside and of a color on the reverse.

## THE ORIGINS OF THE MOTTO

The earliest mottoes probably developed out of famous war cries on the medieval battlefield. Indeed, one of the most famous of all—the English *"Dieu et mon droit"* ("God and my right")—was recorded as having been exclaimed by King Richard the Lionheart at Gisons in 1198. There are plenty of other similar examples, particularly in Scottish and Irish heraldry. The great Irish families of Butler and FitzGerald rallied to their ancient chiefs under the *cris-de-guerre* of "Butler a boo" and "Crom a boo." "A boo" was the Erse cry to victory and "Crom" is a direct reference to Croom Castle, which was an important residence of the FitzGerald family.

In spite of the evidence that suggests some mottoes were derived from battle cries, it is more likely that many originated as an integral part of the heraldic badge. Lots of mottoes use words, in Latin, French, English, or in translation, that are a reference to the family arms themselves. This is known as "canting" or punning on the name, which is examined in detail on pages 192–195. Puns are very popular—*"Cave deus vidit"* ("Beware, God sees") for Cave being one example. Other mottoes are known as "rebus" mottoes, in which the family name appears amongst the words of the inscription or motto. Some of the most clever and allusive of all mottoes combine historical with canting or rebus elements.

## RELIGIOUS CONNOTATIONS

Many heraldic mottoes have a religious import, urging both the bearer and the onlooker to espouse Christian values. One of the best known examples of this is the motto of the great French family of Montmorency, which directly implores God to assist the family with the words *"Dieu ayde au primer baron chrestien."*

## INSCRIPTIONS

Letters and individual words as opposed to complete sentences are often found on armorial shields. These are known as "inscriptions" and, somewhat curiously, are looked down upon by many heraldic experts as being inauthentic. Nonetheless, there are plenty of examples of abbreviations and collections of letters denoting the most elevated of subjects. Perhaps the best known of these is "SPQR" (*Senatus Populusque Romanus*), which was the classic inscription of the Roman empire and which was known throughout the ancient world.

An armorially correct, modern interpretation of a coat of arms, with a blank ribbon placed beneath that is intended for a motto. The crest and heraldic charges emblazoned on the shield are generic and may be replaced as desired. It has been common practice for many years to incorporate a motto ribbon as part of an heraldic design.

# BADGES

BADGES ARE AN ESPECIALLY BRITISH PART OF THE HERALDIC TRADITION, ALTHOUGH THEY HAVE LONG HELD SIGNIFICANCE IN ITALY AS WELL. IN MEDIEVAL BRITAIN MOST COMMON PEOPLE WOULD HAVE RECOGNIZED THE BADGES AND LIVERIES OF THE MAJOR NOBILITY AND THEIR SERVANTS, IF NOT THEIR ACTUAL COATS OF ARMS.

It is quite common to find a badge as part of an achievement of arms. A badge is a simple heraldic device that belongs to the bearer, but which other people can wear in order to show their allegiance to them or their cause.

A badge would be worn by the retainers, messengers, and soldiers of the bearer. In the days when knights held tenure of their lands in exchange for military service, they would come to the battle in their own coat of arms, but also displaying the badge of their overlord, so that nobody was in any doubt as to whom they owed their allegiance. Badges survive today and are worn by military units, fire brigades, police forces, schools and universities, and such like.

Badges are sometimes arranged into the composition of an achievement, so as to be included with it but not form part of it; they may also be found strewn on the compartment or on the mantling of any given design. There is no limit to the subjects that can be used in the design of heraldic badges.

Badges of the St. John family on the tomb of Nicholas St. John. At the top left-hand corner of the image the sun in splendor can be seen, and in the middle there is a fetlock. Various animals adorn the rest of the ceiling.

A selection of modern heraldic badge designs, based on a royal emblem. These are presented on unusual shield shapes and incorporate a number of different classic elements.

# FLAGS AND OTHER ACCESSORIES

MANY DIFFERENT KINDS OF FLAG ARE USED IN HERALDRY, THEIR MAIN PURPOSE BEING TO DISPLAY THE HERALDIC BEARINGS OF THEIR OWNERS, EITHER IN ORDER TO ADVERTISE THEIR PRESENCE OR TO SERVE AS A RALLYING-POINT FOR MEN IN BATTLE. THERE ARE SEVERAL OTHER HERALDIC ACCESSORIES THAT ALSO DESERVE MENTION.

## PENNONS

The pennon was a small triangular flag carried at the tip of a spear by a knight, showing his personal coat of arms. It was made so that the arms were displayed the correct way when he was charging and the spear was level.

## BANNERS

Historically banners are square and display the bearer's arms upon them, as they would be seen on his coat, armor, and shield. Fine examples of these can be seen in St. George's Chapel, Windsor, and Westminster Abbey, where the banners of the present Knights of the Garter and Knights of the Bath, respectively, hang. Any armigerous person can have a banner and fly it from his house when he is present. Banners can also be rectangular, both vertically and horizontally, though in modern parlance the latter shape is generally called a flag. Nowadays most national banners are flag-shaped, like the English Royal Banner, which is universally but quite wrongly called the Royal Standard.

Banners were also used at sea with long streamers of the livery colors. It has been known for arms to be emblazoned on the sails of ships. The Admiral of England in 1436 was the Earl of Huntingdon, who bore on his mainsail the motto, "England within a bordure of France." (A bordure is a narrow band running along the edge of a shield.)

## LIVERY COLORS

It was the custom of those persons who had retainers to dress them in a uniform so that

they could be easily recognized. These uniforms were usually of two colors—usually, though not universally, the chief color and metal of the bearer's arms. The Tudor kings of England had green and white as their livery colors.

A medieval pennon would have looked much like the small triangular flag pictured above. This was an important part of a knight's battle accoutrement, serving as his personal device and clearly displaying his colors while hanging from the end of his spear.

The banners of the present Knights of the Garter, in St. George's Chapel, Windsor.

The banner of the present Knights of the Bath in the Henry VII chapel, Westminster Abbey.

Nuremberg Castle dates from 1050 and includes a splendid painted door displaying the arms of the owner.

## STANDARDS

A standard is a long narrow flag frequently used in heraldry; the longer the flag, the higher the rank of the bearer. It is simply a device for display and pageant, used to present the devices and the livery color of the bearer.

Though the items displayed on standards have varied in the past, nowadays standards show the arms of the bearer next to the pole. The rest of the standard is divided horizontally into the two livery colors. On this is shown the crest, perhaps repeated, the motto on a riband placed diagonally in as many pieces as are needed, and any badge that may have been granted. Standards, like badges, are granted by the relevant heraldic authority to any armigerous person.

## MILITARY COLORS

Military units of all kinds have traditionally carried into battle a banner displaying their badge, their sovereign allegiance, and details of their history and battles. Military colors have always been treated with great respect,

representing as they do the glories and traditions of the regiment. For this reason the colors have been defended with unsurpassed valor in numerous battles. These colors are still proudly displayed today.

## HATCHMENTS

It is quite important to mention hatchments, as they are frequently found in churches, often without any explanation of their meaning.

It used to be the custom to paint the coat of arms of an armiger on a board and hang it up outside his house when he died. This painting would then be carried to the church at the funeral and afterward hung there for all time. In the days before newspapers this was the most practical way of letting everyone know that someone had died. The achievement was always placed on a diamond-shaped board and the style of the composition indicated which member of the household had died. The clue, apart from the heraldic accoutrements, lay in the background of the board, which was painted black behind the arms of the deceased.

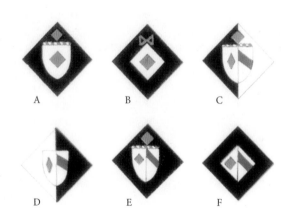

Shown here are the hatchments of: A a dead bachelor;
B a dead spinster; C a dead husband; D a dead wife;
E a dead widower; and F a dead widow.

The funeral brass of Lady Katherine Howard. Her
arms are impaled with those of her husband,
John Howard, Duke of Norfolk.

# ADDITIONS TO ARMS

I N ORDER TO DISTINGUISH FATHER FROM SON—WHEN BOTH WERE WEARING THE SAME HEREDITARY ARMS—HERALDIC SYSTEMS WERE DEVELOPED OVER A PERIOD OF TIME OF ADDING SMALL DISTINGUISHING CHARGES TO THE SHIELD THAT COULD BE REMOVED OR ALTERED AS CIRCUMSTANCES IN THE FAMILY CHANGED.

With the exception of Scottish heraldry, these systems have largely dropped out of use. Scotland has developed a system of adding differently tinted bordures which have to be registered for each member of the family.

Some brothers changed the tinctures on their arms or altered the charges to show that, though related to the original arms, they were in fact different; but this practice, too, has largely fallen into disuse.

The shields of the Black Prince and of his brothers, each displaying the Royal Arms of England but each with a different label, slightly differently charged.

Traditional small marks of difference, added to a coat of arms to denote a junior branch of a family.

Of the 150 or so different designs for the cross, some of the most common are illustrated here.

# MARSHALING OF ARMS

IT IS COMMON TO FIND MORE THAN ONE COAT OF ARMS DISPLAYED ON A SHIELD AND IT IS IMPORTANT TO UNDERSTAND HOW THIS OCCURS. THE PRACTICE OF COMBINING COATS OF ARMS IS KNOWN IN HERALDRY AS "MARSHALING," AND IT IS THIS AREA OF THE SUBJECT THAT MOST PEOPLE FIND HARDEST TO UNDERSTAND.

## IMPALEMENT

This term refers to two coats of arms placed side by side on the same shield. This can happen following a marriage, when the husband's arms appear on the dexter and the wife's on the sinister side of the shield. A person can also impale his arms with the arms of any civic body of which he is the leader, during his tenure of office. The person's arms appear on the sinister and the civic arms on the dexter side of the shield.

## DIMIDIATION

There was a time when only half of each coat of arms was placed on the shield. In some cases this practice produced achievements that were totally unreadable, and it was soon dropped, although some examples still exist that are used to this day.

## QUARTERING

Quartering means dividing the shield into sections, at least four and sometimes as many as twenty-four. In each section a coat of arms is placed that has become permanently joined to the original coat, usually by marriage to an heiress. From the heraldic point of view, an heiress is the daughter of an armiger who has no sons. If there is more than one daughter, they are heiresses jointly and equally. Because there are no sons to carry the arms into the next generation, an heiress who marries an armiger can hand on her arms to her children as a quartering with their father's coat. If her

husband is not an armiger she cannot pass on her arms. If she is already the heiress to a quartered coat she can pass on all or a selection of those quarterings, so long as the quartering that brought them into the family is shown. An even number of quarters is usually shown, repeating the paternal coat in the last quarter if necessary.

Sovereigns also add quarterings to their shields, to demonstrate their sovereignty over different subject states.

## ESCUTCHEON OF PRETENCE

When an armiger marries an heraldic heiress he places her arms, after her father's death, on a small escutcheon in the middle of his shield. When he dies his sons can display their father's coat of arms, quartered with their mother. After a few generations of marriages to heiresses, or to those who subsequently become heiresses because their brothers die, a large number of quarterings can be accumulated. It is important, though often difficult, to distinguish between two quartered coats impaled on the same shield and one multi-quartered coat.

## MARSHALING OF ARMS FOR ORDINARY ARMIGEROUS PEOPLE

When two or more coats of arms are displayed on one shield, especially with respect to royal heraldry, this was done to demonstrate sovereignty over territory. The first point to consider is that heraldry is hereditary. Heraldic

A union of families resulted in an amalgam of arms in
the growing identity of husband and wife in the
identification of their unified estates.

The arms of Sir William Clopton (1591–1618) impaling
those of his first wife, Anne, who was the daughter
of Sir Thomas Barnadiston.

# MARSHALING OF ARMS

Arms of the father.

Arms of his wife who is an heraldic heiress.

The husband bears her arms on his own
as an escutcheon of pretence.

Their heirs may quarter the mother's
arms with those of the father.

Arms of the first-born son. If his mother was
not an heraldic heiress, he bears his father's
arms only with a mark of difference.

# MARSHALING OF ARMS

A MAN WHOSE WIFE IS NOT AN HERALDIC HEIRESS
MAY IMPALE HER ARMS WITH HIS OWN.

Arms of the husband.

His wife's arms impaled with those of his own.

IF A MAN TAKES A POSITION THAT INCLUDES ITS OWN COAT OF ARMS,
HE MAY IMPALE THEM WITH THOSE OF HIS OWN.

Arms of a man before becoming a bishop.

Arms of his see impaled with those of his own.

devices are passed down from one generation to the next.

When a son came of age, he was entitled to display his father's coat of arms, bearing some small "mark of difference" so that it was possible to tell one from the other. When the father died, the first son, who had become the head of the family, removed his mark of difference and bore the "undifferenced" coat of arms of his father. Any other sons retained their marks of difference because their position in the family was unaltered, unless the first son died without his own heir, in which case the next son would take the place as the head of the family and bear the undifferenced coat. These coats of arms could be passed down through the generations in the respective families by the male heirs.

If a man had only daughters his arms could die with him, if none of his daughters married. If there was more than one daughter, they would be heiresses in heraldry of equal right and could display their father's arms after his death until they died, on a lozenge-shaped shield. The arms would then cease to have anyone to bear them and become a matter of history. If, however, one or any of them married, the situation would be different.

If an armigerous man married an heraldic heiress, he could display her arms on an "escutcheon" ("escutcheon of pretence") on his shield. He had no right to the arms, since he would only be preserving them for his heirs. His heirs may then quarter their mother's arms with those of their father. If the parent's arms were each a simple unquartered coat, the form was to divide the shield into four sections and place the paternal coat in the first and fourth quarter and the maternal coat in the second and third quarter. If the mother already had a quartered coat, these quarters would be included in the third and fourth quarter and more if necessary. If the father had a quartered coat, the new quarters came after the last of the father's quarters. It was not necessary to display all the quarters, if there were many, but if any were added the mother's paternal coat must be the first. There would always have to be an even number of quarters and so the paternal coat was repeated in the last quarter if necessary.

If a daughter married a non-armigerous husband, she could display her father's arms until she died, but there was no vehicle for its continuance into the next generation and so the arms died with her. It would be incorrect for her children to display her arms. There was one course open and that was to apply to the College of Arms for a Grant of Arms to the husband in his own right. Once this was done, he could display the wife's arms on his own as an escutcheon of pretence and bear them forward for the next generation.

If a woman had brothers, she was not an heraldic heiress and she could not carry her paternal arms forward, this being already done by her brothers. However, her husband could "impale her arms" (place them side by side on the same shield) with his own. Such arms could not be carried forward by the next generation and the impalement ended with the generation for which it was done. It is still quite common to see arms impaled with civic arms or of other arms pertaining to an office, particularly with bishops, who display the arms of their see on the dexter side of their shield and their paternal arms on the sinister side. If they wished to display their wife's arms as an impalement they would be obliged to marshal together a second shield showing their paternal arms on the dexter side and their wife's paternal arms on the sinister side.

The Turberville window in Bere Regis church in Dorset. The Turberville arms are impaled with those of their many spouses.

This is the coat of arms of Decs, a town in Hungary in the County of Tolna. The coat of arms is marshaled. The chief shield is a heater with a pointed base, quarterly of gules and azure. In the first field gules a Baroque-towered stylized Calvinist church alaisé argent. In the second field azure a leafed bunch of grapes alaisé or. In the third field azure three ears of wheat or, the stalks banded. In the fourth field gules an eight-pointed star argent on the dexter and a man-faced moon increscent argent, both borne alaisé. The inescutcheon is a heater framed or with a pointed base. In the field sable an embroidery motif of Decs alaisé argent.

# AUGMENTATION OF ARMS

THROUGHOUT EUROPE IT HAS BEEN THE PRACTICE OF MONARCHS TO REWARD THEIR SUBJECTS FOR
VALOROUS AND NOBLE DEEDS BY GRANTING TO THEM SOME PERMANENT ADDITION TO THEIR COAT OF
ARMS. THESE TAKE MANY FORMS, BUT THEY ARE USUALLY A CHARGED CANTON, CHIEF, OR ESCUTCHEON OR
EVEN THE IMPALEMENT OF A COMPLETE COAT OF ARMS.

Augmentation of the coat "azure
issuant from the sinister side
a hand and in base a broken
fetlock argent" to be permanently
impaled by the Barons de
Hochpied with their own coat of
"argent between three crescents
sable a chevron gules."

Augmentation of the addition of
a chief of the colors of Belgium to
the de Walters family.

An English augmentation of a
"Canton gules a lion passant or" to
the coat of More—"ermine three
greyhounds courant sable collared
gules."

Augmentation of an unofficial
coat of arms for the Confederation
of Canada, featuring additional
quarterings for provinces that
joined after the four founders.

# The Scottish System of Differencing Arms

The Scottish stsyem for differencing arms for junior branches of the same family calls for permitant additions and alterations to the coat of arms and these must be approved and registered by the appropriate heraldic authorities in Scotland, whose advice should always be sought.

The system is relatively straightforward. From the diagram on the opposite page it will be seen that a father has five sons. The eldest son displays a label that can be removed when he in his turn becomes the head of the family. The other sons difference their arms by employing a different colored bordure. Their sons in turn display the bordure of their father to maintain their differences from the senior branch and in addition they use different lines of partition so that for each one of them, the shield is unique, yet closely related to the original family arms.

An ancient Scottish family coat of arms displayed on a wall within Huntly Castle, Scotland.

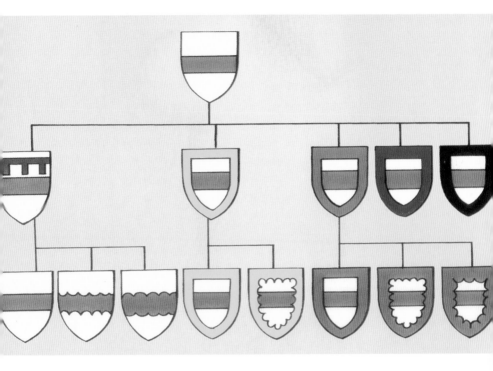

The Scottish system of differencing arms for junior branches of the family.

Unsurprisingly, the blue-and-white saltire design of the Scottish flag features in many arms of that country.

# CHAPTER 4

# SIGNIFICANT SYMBOLS

# ANIMALS

S YMBOLISM IS EVERYTHING IN HERALDRY, AND THE MOST COMMONLY USED CHARGES TO CONVEY A VAST ARRAY OF VISUAL STATEMENTS OF INTENT ARE ANIMALS. THESE COME IN EVERY VARIETY—FROM THE MUNDANE TO THE FANTASTICAL—AND THERE ARE MANY DIFFERENT HERALDIC TERMS TO DESCRIBE THEM AND THEIR POSTURES.

Of all the charges used in heraldry, it is probably animals and mythical beasts that stick most in people's minds. They are extensively used on shields, crests, and badges as well as serving as supporters. Beasts always face the dexter when used as a charge, crest, or badge, unless otherwise stated, and they always look where they are going —that is, to the dexter—again unless otherwise stated. The tail is usually shown erect and curved, in a style according to custom or the discretion of the artist, unless otherwise stated.

There are a number of terms that apply to all animals and monsters, which are collectively classified as "beasts."

ARMED  When applied to beasts, the term "armed" refers to beaks, claws, tusks, horns, and so on. The term usually occurs when these are of a different color from the beast itself, as in "a lion rampant sable, armed gules."
AFFRONTY  Facing the front.
BICORPORATE OR TRICORPORATE  One head with two or three bodies.
CRINED  With a mane or head of hair, separately tinctured.
COWED  With the tail down between the legs.
DEMI  The top half of the body only, usually with tail included.
DISARMED  With no beak, claws, horns, or tusks.
DOUBLE-QUEUED  With two tails.
GUARDANT  Looking at the observer, full-faced, directly out of the shield.
GORGED  With the neck or gorge encircled (by a coronet, for example).

HORNED OR TUSKED  As in "armed," above.
LANGUED  With a tongue of a specified color.
NOWED  Tied in a knot, usually of the tail.
QUEUE FOURCHY OR FOURCHEE  With a forked tail.
REGARDANT  Looking backward.
SINISTER  Facing the other way, to the sinister, as in "a lion rampant sinister."
TUFTED  With tufts of hair.
UNGULED  Of the hoofs of an animal, when their color is different from the color of the body, as in "unicorn argent, unguled or."
VULNED  Wounded and bleeding.

This fierce-looking, standard-bearing lion is displaying a number of the classic aspects of heraldic poses outlined above.

A lion *guardant* has its face toward the viewer.

A lion *double-queued* has two tails.

A lion *demi* is drawn with the top half of the body only, but usually including the tail.

A lion *couchant* is drawn lying down in an alert posture.

A forked tail is called a *queue fourchy*.

A lion looking backward is called *regardant*.

A rather less fierce- and assertive-looking lion in the *regardant* pose.

# PARTS OF THE BODY

In heraldic imagery the head and limbs of animals are frequently found as crests, charges, and badges. These have a variety of special descriptions.

*CABOSHED*  Facing the front and cut off cleanly behind the ears.
*COUPED CLOSE*  Facing the side and cut off cleanly behind the ears.

*COUPED*  Cut off close at the neck—always a clean cut, as if made by a sword.
*ERASED*  As if pulled off, with jagged skin.
*FACE*  A head caboshed.
*JESSANT DE LYS*  A face with a fleur-de-lys positioned behind it and thrust out through the animal's mouth.
*LIMBS*  Paws, arms, legs, and tails are shown couped (cut off close to the body), or erased.

An animal facing the front and cut off cleanly behind the ears is described as *caboshed*.

Each of the animals on this badge is described as *face*, meaning with a head *caboshed*.

An animal facing the side and cut off cleanly behind the ears is described as *couped close*.

*Couped* is the term for any limb cut cleanly off the body.

*Erased* describes any limb drawn as if torn from the body.

The tomb of Richard Berghersh in Lincoln Cathedral. The first and second shields show a lion *queue fourchée* (with a forked tail). The shield of the Suffolk branch of the family was *argent* (white), a *chief gules* (with a red top section covering one third of the shield), overall a lion *rampant queue fourchy or*.

This illustration shows a face *jessant de lys*, with a fleur-de-lys behind, coming through the mouth.

This limb is described as *couped*, as it has been cleanly cut from the body.

This limb is described as *erased*, as it looks as though it has been torn away from the body as opposed to being cut off.

# THE LION—KING OF THE ANIMAL WORLD

Of all the animals the lion is the king. Favored for his nobility and fierceness, the lion has been used in heraldry all over the world. He is always displayed looking as fierce and as haughty as the artist can contrive, with his claws extended. His claws and tongue are always painted red, regardless of what color he is, unless he is on a red field, in which case they are painted blue.

The lion is always shown in one of a variety of set postures, which also apply to other animals. There are a number of terms to describe these postures, outlined below with accompanying illustrations.

Two lions walking in opposite directions are said to be *counter passant*.

**COUCHANT**
Lying down in an alert posture.

**COUNTER PASSANT**
Two lions walking in opposite directions.

**COUNTER SALIENT**
Two lions leaping in opposite directions.

**DORMANT**
Lying down at rest.

**LIONCELLS**
Small lions, usually in large numbers on a shield.

**PASSANT**
Walking across the shield. A lion "passant guardant" is known as a leopard; a leopard of England is a "*lion passant guardant or.*"

**RAMPANT**
Rearing up in fight.

**SALIENT**
Taking a leap across the shield.

**SEJANT**
Sitting on his haunches. When he sits, facing the front, he is termed "*affronty.*"

A lion at rest is *dormant*.

Small lions charged on a shield are called *lioncels*.

Two lions leaping in opposite directions are said to be *counter salient*.

## STATANT
Simply standing there.

## TWO LIONS ADDORSED
Two lions rampant, back to back.

## TWO LIONS RESPECTANT OR COMBATANT
Two lions rampant, face to face.

Lions are frequently found as supporters in coats of arms, in which case they stand holding the shield and, sometimes, the helm as well. It is common to find the head, arm, or paw used as a charge.

It is also common to find lions with collars and chains or with crowns, or carrying something in their paws, or charged on the shoulder with some device. Sometimes they are powdered all over with small charges. There are numerous lion monsters and of these the winged lion and the sea lion are the most common. A lion with a human face and human body and head is also found.

A lion walking across a shield is *passant*; when it is also looking at the observer (*passant guardant*) it is known as a leopard.

A lion rearing up is *rampant*.

*Salient* describes an animal leaping across a shield.

A lion on its haunches is *sejant*.

A lion simply standing, motionless, is described as *statant*.

Two lions *rampant*, back-to-back, are called *addorsed*.

# OTHER POPULAR HERALDIC ANIMALS

Most animals are found in heraldry and since the opening up of the New World all kinds of species unknown to earlier heraldry have been introduced. All of them may appear as supporters, charges, or on crests, in any number of different postures and bearing a wide variety of facial expressions. Some of the most ancient and most common are discussed here.

ABOVE, LEFT TO RIGHT: Heraldic bears often wear a muzzle, derived from their use as performing animals at medieval fairs. The ferocious boar is frequently seen on badges. The badger, often known as a "brock," is also sometimes called a "gray" in heraldic terminology.

BEAR  Usually shown standing upright on his back legs, holding a tree trunk, and often with a muzzle.

BEAVER  Occasionally found in heraldic imagery, usually as a symbol of industry.

BOAR  In medieval times the wild boar was common throughout Europe and regularly hunted. It is always shown with powerful tusks and a crest of bristling hair down its back, usually of a different color. Usually trotting, unless it is a supporter of arms.

BROCK OR BADGER  Occasionally found in all roles. Sometimes also called a "gray".

BUCK (FALLOW DEER)  This animal is distinguished from the stag by its wide, bladed antlers.

BULL  Often encountered, though usually only the head, with a ring in the nose, is shown.

DEER  Species of deer and antelope from the New World are gradually being introduced. Deer have a terminology of their own: when *passant* they are called "trippant"; when *statant guardant*, described as "at gaze"; when *couchant*, "lodged"; when running, "in chase" or "at speed"; and when salient, "springing." Antlers are called "attires" and the points "tines."

ERMINE  A white stoat usually shown as a fur; sometimes found as an animal in its own right.

FOX  The epitome of slyness and cunning, the fox is occasionally found in heraldic imagery.

FROG  The emblem of the devil, the frog is still today associated with witchcraft.

The arms attributed to the devil.

Two breeds of hound—the grayhound and the talbot—are traditionally used in heraldry.

The long, curved horns of the wild bull frequently surmount crests.

The wolf is a rare device in modern heraldry.

GOAT  Always shown in typical billy-goat form, with a rough coat, curved horns, and beard.

HEDGEHOG  Also called an urchin and, in French, an *herrison*.

HORSE  A symbol of speed and bravery, the horse was the emblem of the Saxon kings of England.

HOUND  Though modern breeds of dog are being introduced into heraldry, traditionally only two breeds were used: the grayhound, as an emblem for a swift messenger, and the talbot, an ancient hunting dog somewhere between a hound and a Great Dane, as an emblem of faithfulness.

LAMB  This gentle and acquiescent animal is frequently used as an emblem of Christ.

RABBIT  Also known as a "coney."

RAM  This animal is sometimes found on arms, though not commonly.

SQUIRREL  Usually shown red in color, sitting on its haunches with a nut.

STAG  Normally shown as the red deer, the stag is also called "hart" or "royal" when of a mature age with twelve or more points on the antlers.

TIGER  Modern usage shows the striped animal, as we know it, but in ancient times the "tyger" (as the name is spelt in heraldry) was so far removed from reality as to warrant inclusion among the monsters.

WOLF  Though common throughout Europe in medieval times, this animal is not often found.

# BIRDS

AFTER ANIMALS, BIRDS ARE THE SECOND MOST POPULAR AND IMPORTANT HERALDIC CHARGE. EAGLES WERE PARTICULARLY UBIQUITOUS IN DESIGNS FOR CENTURIES, BUT MANY OTHER LESS EXALTED SPECIES FEATURE IN HERALDIC DEVICES, OFTEN DUE TO THEIR SPECIAL SIGNIFICANCE TO A PARTICULAR FAMILY OR LOCATION.

There are a number of terms that apply to all birds featured in heraldry.

ADDORSED  With the wings back-to-back.

ARMED  Of the color of the claws.

BEAKED  Of the color of the beak, as in a "swan argent beaked gules."

BELLED  Of a falcon, with the falconer's bell attached.

CLOSE  Standing on the ground with wings closed.

CROWNED  With a crown of the specified color on its head.

DISPLAYED  Of a bird placed on the shield affrontly, with both wings and the legs and tail spread out and head turned to the dexter (with two heads, then each looking outward).

DOUBLE-HEADED  With two heads and neck, joined at the shoulders.

ELEVATED  With wing tips pointing upward.

GORGED  With a collar encircling the neck or gorge.

INVERTED  With the wing tips turned down.

JESSED  Of a falcon, with the bell tied on to the leg with a jess.

MEMBERED  Of the color of the legs.

RISING  Of the bird standing on the ground with wings raised.

SOARING  Flying like an eagle or lark.

VOLANT  Flying across the shield.

VULNING  Wounding.

A German royal coat of arms featuring a "displayed" double-headed black eagle with wings spread.

Crests commonly feature ostrich feathers, as does the famous badge of the Prince of Wales.

Addorsed

Displayed

Double-headed

Inverted

Rising

Soaring

# THE PRINCIPAL BIRDS OF HERALDRY

An extraordinary array of birds features in heraldry across the world. The eagle was associated with empires from Roman times and the brave black eagle was a particular favorite of both Byzantine and Holy Roman emperors for centuries. In addition to the many different real species discussed below, fanciful and fantastic creations such as the footless and beakless martlet featured in many designs. This swift-like creature was reputedly seen in the Holy Land by the Crusaders and was believed by medieval writers never to land on the ground, forever staying in flight.

OWL  This ubiquitous bird often appears in heraldry as a crest and a charge, and more often than not as a symbol of wisdom and learning.

SWAN  Images of this bird are frequently found in heraldry. In England this is a royal bird and accordingly it has been used for centuries as a charge, supporter, and badge.

PEACOCK  This beautiful and exotic-looking bird has long been a symbol of royalty in eastern countries.

PELICAN  In heraldry this bird is often depicted as a female, tearing at her own breast in order to feed her young. This practice of wounding with the beak is known as "vulning," and a pelican engaging in such an activity is referred to as a "pelican in her piety." For this reason, such a symbol of self-sacrifice is often found in religious coats of arms.

MARTLET  This mythical bird, which frequently appears as a charge in arms, is thought to represent the swift. It was believed that because it was so common in the Holy Land, it became an emblem of someone who had been on pilgrimage.

DOVE  Normally shown carrying a laurel branch, this bird has become an internationally known emblem of peace and hope. However, in heraldry it is far more likely that it will be drawn standing, with a small crest, and it may or may not have one wing raised. As such it will be found on the arms of the College of Heralds in England. The Egyptians understood the homing instinct of the bird and used it to carry messages. It could be that this charge alludes to the herald's role in carrying messages for his master, across frontiers, unhindered.

BITTERN  This appears as the crest of Barnadiston (see opposite) and is drawn stalking between bullrushes. However, it has a more characteristic head-down pose, which it adopts when it is seeking to remain undiscovered.

COCK  Like many other things, the cock appeared in art and symbolism long before heraldry was established as a recognizable art form. In Christian art, it is employed as a sign of the call to repentance. As foretold, St. Peter denied Jesus three times before the cock crowed and it appears on top of many Christian churches in the form of a weather vane. Due to its extreme pugnacity, in heraldry the cock is often employed by military persons.

CORMORANT  An emblem of sea power, this bird makes frequent appearances in heraldry.

STORK  This bird is often shown standing on one leg, holding a stone in its other foot. Drawn in this way, it is known as a "stork in her vigilance." The idea is that if the stork falls asleep it will drop the stone onto its other foot and wake up with a start!

Owl

Swan

Peacock

Pelican

Martlet

Dove

Bittern (Crest of Barnadiston)

Bittern

Stork in her vigilance

LAPWING  Tyrwhitt bears gules, three tyrwhitts (peewits) or.

MOORCOCK  In heraldry you will often see this bird drawn looking like a cockerel, with two stiff tail feathers sticking straight out, which would describe it as a "heraldic moorcook." The moorcook is in fact the blackcock and perhaps a more realistic rendition, whilst endeavoring to maintain the heraldic postures and ideal, might be more apt.

GROUSE, CAPERCALLIE, PHEASANT, AND PARTRIDGE  The Worshipful Company of Cooks displays a pheasant as a crest and Partridge displays gules three partridges proper.

PARROT, EMU, OSTRICH, AND OTHER EXOTIC BIRDS  These birds all appear as emblems or supporters for people who are working overseas. The ostrich has appeared in heraldry since the earliest times and—because of its pugnacious nature at certain times of the year and its habit of eating indigestible objects—this symbol has been used by fighting men.

PENGUIN AND ALBATROSS  These seabirds appear for those who have ventured into southern waters, although the albatross has the additional attribute in heraldry of being applicable to someone who has wandered far from home.

GUILLIMOT AND DUCKS OF DIFFERENT KINDS  These birds invariably appear as supporters in many coats of arms.

HERON  When herons are depicted, it is normally in relation to fishing rights. They are occasionally depicted with objects in their beaks.

CHOUGH  This small black bird is similar in size and confirmation to the jackdaw, although it is black all over with a red beak and legs. In England it is associated particularly with Cornwall, where it can be widely found.

SMALL BIRDS  In addition to larger and more well-known birds, some small and relatively insignificant birds also appear quite frequently in heraldic imagery.

CROW  Crows, known as corbies, are displayed by a family of that name.

EAGLE  Eagles have been used for centuries as a symbol of empire. The eagle is widely regarded as the king of the bird kingdom, just as the lion holds sway over all the other creatures in the world of animals. Throughout heraldry there are many examples of eagles preying on other creatures, as well as examples of eagles' legs and heads used as charges. In German heraldry, the displayed eagles' wings often appear in pairs as a crest.

FALCONRY  This was a very important sport and method of obtaining food throughout the Middle Ages, and Greenland falcons, gyrfalcons, peregrines, and goshawks were all widely captured and trained to hunt. Falcons often appear in heraldry, and are usually depicted "jessed and belled." The falcon wore a small bell on its leg fastened with thin leather jesses, so that the falconer could find it by listening out for it should it alight in a wood. Falcon bells appear as charges, as do the little hat or hood that was traditionally put on the falcon's head to keep the bird sitting quietly on the falconer's hand. The falconer could bring a falcon back to his hand by whirling a lure (a piece of meat) around his head. Happily, this ancient sport is enjoying a considerable revival today and many people have a chance to see these majestic birds flying in demonstrations at country fairs and elsewhere. Ironically, this most ancient of sports has also found a new lease of life via that most modern of machines, the jet aircraft. Damage to highly expensive jet engines is being caused by birds being sucked in at take off and landing. The potential for catastrophe is enormous and so airfields now regularly employ falconers to keep flocks of gulls, lapwings, starlings, and pigeons away from airfields.

Heraldic moorcock

Moorcock

Eagle's leg

Eagle's head (erased)

Falcon

Lure

# FISH AND SHELLS

Fish is a broad term in heraldry, as the dolphin and the whale are both classified as such, even though they are of course mammals. The dolphin is the most commonly occurring sea creature in heraldry, probably due to its size, although ferocious fish were often preferred by medieval heralds as well.

## THE FISH

All kinds of fish appear in heraldry, with the pike, sardines, and perch being especially popular. Many of the general animal postures described earlier apply equally to fish, but there are also some heraldic terms that apply specifically to them.

EMBOWED  Formed in a graceful curve, usually like that of a dolphin.

NAIANT  Swimming across the shield, heads to the dexter.

HAURIENT  Swimming up to the top of the shield.

URINANT  Swimming down to the bottom of the shield. Fish are frequently used in arms to allude to the name of the bearer and they sometimes appear of no specified type. They can be used as charges and crests. The crest of the Solomon Islands, for example, has an alligator and a shark haurient as supporters and that of the Bahamas bears a swordfish and a flamingo.

## THE SHELLS

The escallop is the most commonly used shellfish, and frequently denotes that the bearer has been on a pilgrimage or is a pilgrim in the metaphorical sense of the word. Three escallop shells on a shield cannot be taken to mean that the bearer has been on three pilgrimages. Whelk shells also appear.

ABOVE RIGHT: The common postures of heraldic fish.

RIGHT: The escallop is a more common shell in heraldry than the whelk.

Embowed

Naiant

Haurient

Urinant

Demi-luce

Escallop

Whelk

An heraldic gable in west Frisia, Netherlands, featuring both fish and shells in the design.

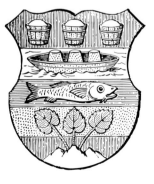

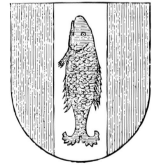

This is the coat of arms of the City of Glasgow in Scotland, featuring a prominent fish with a large ring in its mouth.

The highly aquatic coat of arms of the town of Gmunden in Austria.

The coat of arms of Kaiserslautern in Germany features a large fish.

# INSECTS AND REPTILES

INSECTS AND REPTILES ARE RARER THAN OTHER BEASTS IN MEDIEVAL HERALDRY, ALTHOUGH THE BEE HAS LONG BEEN HELD AS A SYMBOL OF INDUSTRY AND GENERAL "BUSYNESS." HOWEVER, IN RECENT YEARS ALL KINDS OF SNAKES, CROCODILES, AND A VARIETY OF INSECTS HAVE BECOME INCREASINGLY POPULAR IN HERALDIC DESIGNS.

## HERALDIC TERMINOLOGY

Once again, there are a number of ancient heraldic terms that apply specifically to insects and reptiles, despite their relative obscurity in the art form. Although lizards and snakes do appear as charges on occasion, they are not very common. Other reptiles are rare, though there are many modern examples of crocodiles. In all cases, the following distinctive terms apply:

NOWED Knotted, when used in conjunction, for example, with the tail of a snake or lizard. The term and accompanying visual imagery convey the twisted, slippery nature of serpents.
COILED With the head erect and in a posture ready to strike, such as when applied to a cobra.
GLISSANT Meaning "gliding," this term is most commonly applied to birds in heraldry but is sometimes also used in connection with insects and flying reptiles.

Bees have traditionally been used in heraldry and are also favored in modern designs, like this one by Debra Hughes.

KHOTSO  PULA  NALA

Although heraldry originated hundreds of years ago and is widely viewed as a primarily medieval, European phenomenon, its rich symbolism and the power of its visual imagery remain undimmed in many modern designs. This is the coat of arms and seal of the southern African kingdom of Lesotho, prominently featuring a crocodile at its heart, a creature that is indelibly associated with Lesotho's national identity.

# PLANTS AND FLOWERS

THE USE OF FLOWERS AND PLANTS IN HERALDRY IS SO WIDESPREAD AND SIGNIFICANT THAT THESE SUBJECTS MAKE A SPECIAL AND FASCINATING STUDY ALL OF THEIR OWN, FULL OF INSPIRING MATERIAL BORROWED FROM THE SYMBOLISM AND CULTURE OF OTHER EARLIER TRADITIONS AND IDEALS.

Herein lies one of the strengths and charms of heraldry and a possible clue as to why the art has endured and indeed flourished for so long after its actual usage has passed. Heraldry is able to assimilate and adapt symbolism from all walks of life and can use and incorporate ideas that reflect all aspects of that life—past, present, and in the future. There is no limit to what might be incorporated into heraldic symbolism and this is to the enduring benefit of the art.

The plants and flowers found so abundantly in creation are equally abundantly used in heraldry, in their magnificent and plentiful variety. But how can it be that these beautiful and completely unbellicose objects should find themselves part of the tools of an art that derived its necessity from warfare?

## HOW FLOWERS FIRST CAME TO HERALDRY

It is true that heraldry as we know it today has evolved over the centuries and that many of the devices employed have come from other and earlier civilizations and artistic concepts. This evolution was considerably boosted by the efforts of the early Christian knights to rid the Holy Land of the invading Turks and by the fact that warfare had developed at the same time to the stage when the knights were so encased in chain mail and armor that it was impossible to tell who was who. The need for a plainly visible scheme of personal identification was very real.

If the basic need was a military one, why then choose a rose, that emblem of love? It would hardly strike terror into the heart of the

foe. Far better to choose a lion to show how fierce you were or a severed head to show what happened to your adversaries.

There must have been some reason why these beautiful emblems, on the face of it more suited to decorate a ladies boudoir than a shield of war, were chosen. The reason was most likely the force that was medieval Christian religion.

## THE POWER OF MEDIEVAL CHRISTIANITY

In order to explore that reason, we must first look more deeply into the ethos of medieval society. Without question the great dominating factor of the age, the pendulum of the life of the time, the mainspring of motivation, was Christianity and the Christian way of life. Look at the wonderful ecclesiastical buildings that still stand today, erected as long ago as in the 12th, 13th, 14th, and 15th centuries all over Europe. Relatively few domestic buildings of that age survive. It was obviously more important for a successful person to endow a magnificent and enduring church in the hope that the pious act might help his immortal soul, than to provide for his bodily comfort whilst still living.

The fantastic works of art that remain to us from those days are nearly all of a religious nature. People gave their lives for and to the Christian ideal, as is witnessed by the crusades, the orders of chivalry, and the great monastic institutions, some of which remain to this day.

People hoped that they would go to the Holy Land before they died, and some of the earlier orders of knights were made up of people,

# THE PRINCIPAL FLOWERS IN HERALDRY

LILY—THE QUEEN OF THE PLANTS IS DEPICTED EITHER AS THE STYLIZED FLEUR DE LYS, WHICH IS DESIGNED IN A VARIETY OF DIFFERENT FORMS, OR AS THE NATURAL FLOWER

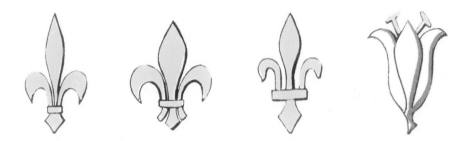

Many stylized versions of the lily are found in heraldry.

ROSE—THE ROSE IS THE QUEEN OF THE FLOWERS. IT IS NEARLY ALWAYS SHOWN IN A STYLIZED FORM, THE HERALDIC ROSE. "SLIPPED AND LEAVED PROPER," WHICH APPLIES TO OTHER FLOWERS AS WELL AS THE ROSE, MEANS THAT THE OUTER GREEN SEPALS AND THE LEAVES ARE SHOWN ON A SHORT LENGTH OF GREEN STALK. "SEEDED" REFERS TO THE COLORS OF THE CENTER

The heraldic rose is nearly always shown in a stylized form. The Tudor Rose of England (right) amalgamates the red rose of the House of Lancaster and the white rose of the House of York.

often younger sons, without much hope of any inheritance from home, who gave up everything to assist and defend these pilgrims on their journey. As the threat to the holy places from the invasions of the Turks increased, Orders of Knights were established to defend them as best they could and many lost their lives in the conflicts that followed.

## THE CRUSADES

When the Turks finally overran Jerusalem and the Christians were driven out, the popes of that time called the crusades. They offered, by the power that had been handed down to them from the Savior himself through the successors of St. Peter, plenary indulgences, complete remission, and forgiveness of all sin, a free pass straight into heaven to any who died attempting to liberate the Holy Lands, so that Christian pilgrims might visit them once more. Parties of knights went from all over Europe, hoping that they might succeed, but assured that if they failed they would achieve their life's ambition and be able to stand in the presence of God. The crusades drew knights from all over Europe who went in groups, selecting their own personal emblems, but all displaying the cross in one of its many forms on their banners, and on the shoulders of their cloaks. Of course there were many, as in any ideological conflict, who went along for the adventure, for the fight, or for what they could earn or grab for themselves, but even among those there were some who hedged their bets and selected religious-type emblems, just in case!

It would be quite wrong to suggest that every emblem in heraldry had a religious significance and most, quite plainly, have none at all. Some express sovereign prowess or domination. Some show bellicose intent, some are allusive to the arms of an overlord, or have some connection to the name of the bearer. Some allude to occupation or office, but some, just a few, are a puzzle and this certainly applies to flowers and flower-like objects. Since, on the surface, flowers seem unsuitable for heraldry (most unlikely to strike terror into the heart of an enemy), there

must be some higher reason for why they are so commonly used. Most likely it is that they were religious emblems, perfectly understood by people of the time, and were chosen to invoke divine protection for the bearer. Medieval Christianity probably had a far greater effect on people than is widely considered today.

## RELIGIOUS REFORMATION

The religious ethos of our times has been largely shaped by events that took place in the 16th century. A great wave of reforming protest swept through Europe and much that was important and vital before that time was deliberately dismantled and destroyed. Through the gradual secularization of the years this has been all but forgotten. However, there is no doubt that the church was in need of reformation and that it had assumed a role and temporal powers that were completely at odds with its foundation. Popes and bishops had set themselves up as kings and princes and they held power over all the kings of western Europe. They held tenure over land in every kingdom and had accrued temporal wealth that ignored the tenants of the Savior. They forgot that "He had come to serve, not to rule" and that His Kingdom was not of this world, but of the next. They forgot that when He sent His apostles out, He told them to take nothing and that theirs was the care of souls. They knew the path to heaven and it was their role to show it to others.

So much of the money and land donated by the wealthy in the hope of expiation of their temporal wrongs and the salvation of their immortal souls was used to establish a temporal state that was powerful enough to dominate the whole of western Europe. Unfortunately, as is often the case, when the Reformation came it swept aside the good, the bad, and the ugly alike. The bad, the rotten apples in the barrel, caused the good to be rejected with the dross and much of what had gone before—people's faiths, beliefs, and ideals—were swept aside by men who, however noble their intent, had deliberately cut themselves off from the spiritual

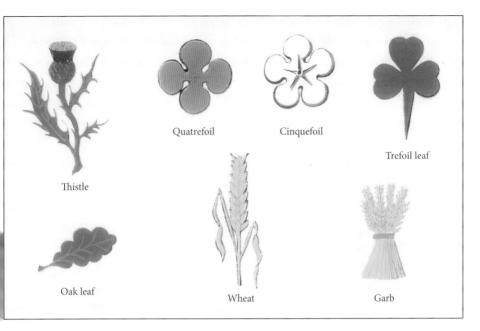

Quatrefoil

Cinquefoil

Trefoil leaf

Thistle

Oak leaf

Wheat

Garb

There are many stylized shapes of flower in heraldry, which are often connoted by the number of petals or the specific shape of the flowerhead or the overall plant.

guidance of the Savior that had been handed down in succession through the centuries.

From that time on the Christian ethos declined in western Europe and was gradually replaced by religions that derived their authority from their human founders. Unfortunately, much of the symbolism and ecclesiastical art and decoration were destroyed at the same time and many of the ideals of religious symbolism became forgotten and derided.

## SYMBOLISM IN HERALDIC FLOWERS

There are a number of highly developed and carefully stylized designs and forms in the depiction of flowers and plants in heraldic imagery. These most likely held largely religious symbolism, although there is much historical debate about the specific meaning of some. The following are some of the most important.

TREFOIL  St. Patrick used the three lobes of the plant that made up each leaf to demonstrate to the people of Ireland the doctrine of the Holy Trinity. This plant has therefore become an emblem of the Holy Trinity, or indeed of any situation that is, or has been, composed of three parts. St. Patrick later became the patron saint of Ireland, and the shamrock has become the national emblem. It is often used to allude to all things and people Irish.

QUATREFOIL  There are many examples of the quatrefoil in heraldry and it is usually described as a flower of four petals. The most conspicuous flower of four petals is the poppy and there is no doubt that this could have been the model for this device. However, it is hard to imagine that when this flower was brandished at an enemy who was bent on death and mayhem, it was especially likely to send him running in terror!

It would have been more likely to evoke his derision and, worse still, if in telling of it afterward he decided that the quatrefoil was supposed to represent a pansy.... The quatrefoil has also been described as a cross made of leaves, and it would seem that this might be nearer the truth. There are many different examples of crosses used in heraldry and this just may be another. It may also represent the sign of the cross, made by the user, expressing that what he is about to do is done to the greater glory of God and invoking divine protection and guidance.

The trefoil and quatrefoil shapes are often to be seen in the decorative treatment of churches, especially in the stonework in windows and the woodwork of beams, screens, and pews. It could be just pure coincidence that these elegant shapes, so suited to occupy the spaces provided by the design of such things, have been used. It could be that these devices are so sympathetic to use in design that they are among that group of natural items which have emerged from the mists of time as being amongst the most perfect of decorations. It could also be that the designers of the churches were taking every chance that they could of reminding the observer of some of the basic tenets of the Christian faith. How much more we would know if the painted decorations of our churches had been preserved and they had not been covered over in purifying white by those who, in seeking to return to a simpler, more uncluttered religion, destroyed, removed, or simply threw them away.

CINQUEFOIL  This is often described as a stylized, five-leafed or petaled flower, and there are many flowers that it could be said to represent.

OCTOFOIL  There are no six- or seven-leafed foils and so the existence of this charge must evoke some attention. What is the significance of eight? If there is any credence in the idea of these emblems being based in Christian symbolism, it does not take long to discover that the octofoil must be the representation of the Beatitudes, those great virtues explained by

Jesus in what has now become known as the Sermon on the Mount. This was a single symbol that expresses all the ideals and aspirations of those who were prepared to dedicate their lives to helping others in the service of God.

HERALDIC ROSE  The heraldic rose is drawn to look like the wild rose of the hedgerows and is shown with a single row of petals and with yellow seed heads in the center. Indeed, it has been described by some as the exact representation of the hedgerow flower. In England they think of the rose in patriotic terms—the English Rose, the Tudor Rose, the national emblem, and so on. But are things as obvious as they might appear? The well-known and well-loved Tudor Rose came into use sometime after the marriage of Henry VII of England and Elizabeth of York as a symbol of the final unity of these two warring factions that had been at each other's throats for nigh on 100 years. If we are to believe the Shakespearean version of the story, each party plucked a rose from a bush and declared it his emblem and the emblem of those who supported him and his House. These roses remained the emblems of the two factions until the subsequent strife ended. The House of Lancaster sported a red rose and that of York, white. Display of a red or white rose indicated support for one party or the other. However, the rose was in use as a heraldic charge long before the events of the Wars of the Roses took place. Therefore, some earlier explanation is needed as to why this object was chosen as an emblem that might serve its wearer in battle. Some research into Christian symbolism will produce a possible answer. An answer that we would all know, understand, and accept, had it not been for the Reformation and consequent events in England. The rose was an especial symbol of the Virgin Mary. Such has been the secularization of Christianity in this country and the erosion of faith in the face of rationalism that devotion to Her has been relegated almost to the level of a superstition. People forget, or do not know, that there was a time when this country was proud to call itself "the Dowry of Mary."

The Royal Badge of the United Kingdom of Great Britain and Northern Ireland features a prominent heraldic rose which is actually a composite of the white rose of the House of York and the red rose of the House of Lancaster.

Two shields in the stone of Lincoln Cathedral; The Farr shield (left) shows a saltar with four fleur-de-lis. The shield of Weller (right) displays three roses.

A devotion to the Blessed Mother of God grew in England to a level that was unique in the western world. How this developed is not known for sure, but it almost certainly evolved from the appearance of the Blessed Virgin to Lady Richolds at Walsingham in the reign of Edward the Confessor. The Virgin Mary, in a vision to that lady, asked her to build a copy of the house in Nazareth. She assured her that all who visited there to honor the fact that an angel of the Lord appeared to a virgin maiden to tell her that she was chosen to be the mother of the Son of God, would have their prayers answered. The shrine was built in 1061 and in the centuries that followed it became the most important pilgrimage place in the Christian world, next to Jerusalem. The devotion to Our Lady spread all over England, as is witnessed by the number of other shrines that were built and the number of churches that were dedicated to her patronage. This devotion continued in the country until 1538, when Henry VIII, instead of nationalizing what would have been a good source of revenue, ordered the destruction of the shrine at Walsingham. This set in train a series of events that ensured that devotion to Our Lady was removed from the national religion.

The great prayer to the Mother of God is called the rosary. This contemplative prayer consists of five parts, each part symbolized by one of the five petals of the rose from which it takes its name. Each one of the petals also stands for one of the five letters MARIA. The string of beads upon which this devotion is counted is also called a rosary.

The saying of the rosary is a meditation upon the life of Our Lady and a supplication for her intercession through her Son, to the Father, for one's earthly difficulties. Each of the five parts of this prayer consider a different episode in Our Lady's life. These episodes, or Mysteries, as they have become called, are represented by different

The arms of Astley of Norfolk on Norwich Cathedral, showing a cinquefoil ermine pierced in the first quarter.

colored roses: the Glorious Mysteries by a yellow rose; the Joyful Mysteries by a white rose; and the Sorrowful Mysteries by a red rose.

Mary has a unique and much misunderstood place in the mediation between man and God which is the reason for the great devotion to her. It seems natural then for a medieval knight, about to embark on an adventure to free the Holy Lands, to display on his shield a token of supplication to one who could intercede to God on his behalf. Unfortunately, while this may be the origin of the use of the rose in heraldry, it does not help us with the model for the flower itself.

It seems that medieval gardens were not much different to our own and from such illustrations as are available they seemed to consist of small walled enclosures—as much to keep wild animals out as to provide shelter for the plants and occupants. It appears that the flowers and plants illustrated were often of an allegorical nature, telling stories to those who understood, and so cannot be taken as reliable indications of what actually might have grown there. However, they do mostly include rose bushes. The space in such a garden must, of necessity, have been limited, and it seems unlikely that much would have been given over to the cultivation of a plant that grew in parks, woods, and forests and which was almost immune to the ravages of grazing animals. A search through works on the subject of roses reveal that the single red rose was brought back to this country by Edmund Langley, son of Edward I. He was at that time Duke of Lancaster. Apparently, he brought it back from a punitive expedition to the south of France, where it had become established via returning crusaders. The religious significance of all this to the medieval mind can be readily seen, as can its choice for the Lancastrian emblem. This red rose can still be found and is known today as *Rosa gallica*. The white rose, also, is not native to this country. It was apparently introduced to England by the Romans and is still available today, and botanically known as *Rosa alba*.

LILY  Much has been written about the lily and it has become accepted as the emblem of purity. As such it has been used as an emblem for Our Lady and for her husband, St. Joseph. It is also used as an emblem for St. Anthony. In heraldry it is generally depicted as being white.

FLEUR-DE-LYS  There are many theories about the origin of this charge and about what it is supposed to represent. It has been extensively used as an emblem in French heraldry and has been associated with the royal house. Legend has it that it was given to Clovis, king of France, by St. Denis. Others say that his soldiers plucked the flower and wore it in their hats. Yet more say that his soldiers waved it in the air when wading through a dense reedy marsh so that they could see each other. Most seem to agree that it is an heraldic representation of the yellow marsh "flag" or iris. Care should be taken not to confuse it with the lily.

COLUMBINE  Columbine is the floral emblem of the third person of the Holy Trinity, the manifestation of the power of God active in the world, known as the Holy Spirit. The flower of the columbine so resembles a group of doves (representations of the Spirit of God) drinking round a bowl that it is easy to see how it got its name and how it was accepted as the flower of the Holy Spirit. In addition, the six points of the flower and the stalk making seven, are the same as the number of the gifts of the Holy Spirit: wisdom, understanding, counsel, fortitude, knowledge, piety, and fear of the Lord.

DAISY  This flower, which is rarely seen in heraldry, represents humility.

SUNFLOWER  As well as representing the sun, being gold in color it also represents money, wealth, and good fortune.

LOTUS  This flower has been brought into heraldry in association with people who have had connections with the Far East.

PALM  This represents martyrdom, either in fact or to an ideal.

LAUREL  These leaves are an ancient emblem of valor and victory. They were much favored by the ancient Romans.

OAK LEAVES  These are used to represent valor and steadfastness.

## INTERPRETING SYMBOLS

These are just some of the plants and flowers used in heraldry. There is no limit to those that might be used in given circumstances and many are used that have a punning or allusive connotation to the bearer or his name, situation, or circumstance.

While it is interesting to speculate about what symbols mean and to muse upon how such unlikely things come to be incorporated into heraldry, it must be remembered that times and language change. We can only surmise about what things must have meant to the medieval person in the light of such information as we can glean. It is important to remember that language had a completely different meaning 1,000 years ago and so the use of our modern terms may give us completely the wrong clues.

Interesting though it may be to try and deduce the possible meaning of such things, it does not help that much in the study of heraldry. There may be several different reasons why a particular person has, say, a rose on his shield and in all probability none of them have anything to do with Our Lady. Though in our time, items on shields are chosen with great care and a great deal of research and thought goes into the granting of devices to an aspirant armiger today, the observer can deduce little from looking at the achievement. We can speculate as to why it has been so assembled, but we may well be wrong.

The white rose of Yorkshire shares a special significance in English heraldry with the red rose of Lancaster, being a composite part of the national emblem.

The fleur-de-lys has a special significance in many areas of heraldry, particularly that of French royalty.

Fleur-de-lys come in a variety of different shapes and designs and are often repeated in multiples as patterns.

# MYTHICAL BEASTS

MONSTERS IN HERALDRY ARE THE PRODUCT PARTLY OF MYTHOLOGY AND LEGEND, PARTLY OF FERTILE IMAGINATIONS, AND PARTLY OF IGNORANCE. HERALDIC ARTISTS COMPOSED DESIGNS OF CREATURES THAT THEY HAD NEVER SEEN, BASED ON THE TALES OF TRAVELERS WHO REPEATED STORIES HEARD IN FAR-OFF LANDS.

However the mythical beasts were created, they offered medieval heralds perhaps the most colorful devices for heraldic expression. In the days when the drama and pageant of the tournament and its attendant fairs and entertainments provided the main excitement of the age, the opportunity for display which monsters gave the heralds was eagerly seized. Someone trying to devise a costume to be worn by his pages as they paraded his shield around the arena had a vast field to exploit once the idea of heraldic monsters took hold. Think of the costume possibilities for someone trying to express the idea that he was as fierce as a lion, strong as an ox, swift as a horse, and cunning as a fox!

The monsters, which, with a few differences, all follow the rules and customs of the animals, fall into several different groups.

WINGED ANIMALS These are ordinary animals given wings to lend them a greater mythological significance, like the winged lion of St. Mark, the winged horse, Pegasus, and so on.

SEA ANIMALS Many animals, especially the lion and the horse, are turned into sea monsters by giving them fish tails or fins.

DRAGON The dragon is a four-legged monster with thick, scaly skin-like armor, a long tail ending with a sting, bat-like wings, and a horned head with a forked tongue, prominent teeth, and claws. He can be of any color and is a consistently popular charge in heraldry.

PHOENIX This mythical bird is essentially an eagle, with a tuft on its head, rising from the flames, as legend has it.

SALAMANDER This is a lizard, sitting in flames, completely unhurt.

UNICORN A horse with a long single horn on its head, the unicorn is an animal of great beauty and allure.

WYVERN This is, in effect, a two-legged dragon. When blazoned properly this creature is green with a red chest and belly and red underwings.

Winged monsters—these are griffins or gryphons—came in a wide variety of different shapes, sizes, and postures.

This stylized emblem of Wales features elements that pre-date the English conquest of the 15th century, with two matching and highly detailed dragon supporters to the fore.

A thoroughly modern rendition of traditional heraldic griffins, supporting a stylized shield. Griffins, dragons, and wyverns have been used in many different areas of heraldic design for hundreds of years.

The chained porcupine crest of the Countess of Sussex, on her tomb in Westminster Abbey. Of course, these animals are not strictly monsters, but they would have been rarely known in medieval times and are depicted "monstrously"!

## MONSTERS COMPOSED OF MORE THAN ONE ANIMAL

Many mythical creatures of medieval heraldry combined the characteristics of two or more known animals, in an attempt to ascribe multiple qualities to the bearer of arms. The vivid imaginations of the medieval heralds led to some truly fantastical creations.

**BONICON**  A bull/horse with curled horns, this creature is useless for attack, but breaks wind with such effect as to devastate several acres behind him.

**COCKATRICE OR BASILISK**  This creature is a wyvern with a cockerel's head.

**ENFIELD**  This has a fox's head, a wolf's body, tail, and back legs, and an eagle's front legs.

**GRIFFIN OR GRYPHON**  This ubiquitous monster has the head, breast, wings, and foreclaws of an eagle and the body, tail, and hind legs of a lion. It also has pointed ear tufts. The griffin is a very strong monster and should always be drawn as such, combining the characteristics of the eagle, king of the birds, with those of the lion, king of the beasts.

**HERALDIC ANTELOPE**  This has a lion's body and tail, a dragon's head with long serrated horns, and the legs and hooves of a deer.

**HERALDIC TYGER**  The tyger resembles a lion in form, but with a longer snout, turned-down horn on the end, and tusks in the lower jaw. He is usually colored bright red. He is also very swift and notoriously hard to catch.

**OPINICUS**  This creature is the same as a griffin, but with four lion's legs.

**OUNCE**  This is a mythical beast resembling the leopard. In heraldry it is sometimes shown as a black panther.

**PANTHER**  This creature resembles the real animal in form, but is usually colored white and covered with multi-colored spots. This monster is always shown as incensed, that is, with flames issuing from its ears and mouth. Some people argue that these are in fact the sweet breath which excites other animals, but puts the fear of death into dragons, on whom the panther preys.

**YALE**  The yale has the body and legs of a goat, a long nose, and tusks like those of a boar. He has two curving horns, which swivel in any direction to fend off attack. One horn is usually shown pointing forward, the other backward.

The ounce, a mythical beast resembling a leopard, often appears in heraldry as a black panther, as shown in the coat of arms pictured above.

# MONSTERS COMPOSED
# OF HUMAN BEINGS

The medieval heralds' lively imaginations did not stop at monsters made up of hybrid animals! In addition to mythical beasts comprised of various creatures, the artists contrived monsters that were part-animal, part-human. Some exceedingly weird and wonderful assemblages were the result, but they always looked interesting on the various arms that they graced.

CENTAUR This creature has the body and legs of a horse joined to the torso of a man.

HARPY The harpy is definitely a creature not to be lightly displayed. They have been described as hags whose duty it was to snatch away the souls of the dead and carry them away to the gods. They were reputed to be very fierce and would slay any man that they met but were filled thereafter with remorse. They are depicted in a variety of ways. An eagle with a man's face. The same with a woman's face. In the arms of the city of Nuremberg, a harpy is depicted with a crowned woman's face and torso and eagle's legs, tail, and wings.

MANDRAKE This is the head of a man with a poisonous root attached to it. The mandrake is in fact a plant with a knobbly root, which is said to resemble the human figure. It is said to let out such a shriek when pulled out of the ground that it makes all those who hear it deaf. It is attributed with considerable medical properties and though rarely used in heraldry in England, it is more common on the Continent.

MELUSIN This is a variant of the mermaid, which is depicted with two tails that she holds in each hand. She is more common in continental heraldry. She is sometimes said to have snakes' tails, but is usually depicted with those of fishes.

MERMAID Fabulous creatures of the deep, that might lure those foolhardy enough to venture upon the seas to a watery grave by their desirable beauty, mermaids have been a part of the legends of man ever since the first sailor settled in front of the evening fire and told with misty eye the perils of his adventures. It used to be the belief that every creature on the land had its counterpart in the sea and so sea dogs, sea lions, sea horses, sea wolves, and sea men and women were perfectly acceptable creatures. A mermaid is always depicted as a beautiful woman with a fish tail from the navel downward. She is usually shown looking into a mirror and combing her hair.

MERMAN This is a male mermaid. The merman appears rarely and, as he is a frightening creature, is not often used. He has no special attributes and can be shown holding anything or nothing. He is sometimes dressed in armor.

SAGITTARY This weird creature has the body and limbs of a lion joined to the torso, arms, and head of a man.

SPHINX This is not a very common charge in heraldry. It takes two forms: the Greek sphinx is shown winged with the face and bust of a woman and the body of a lion; the Egyptian sphinx has the face of a man in the head-dress of a pharoah and the body of a lion and is always shown couchant.

TRITON This is a merman holding a trident and blowing into a shell trumpet. He is occasionally shown in armor, as on the arms of the Worshipful Company of Fishmongers in London. When the merman holds a trident and has a conch shell, through which he can blow up a storm, he becomes a Triton.

MANTICORE OR MANTYGER This creature, which is fairly rare in its appearances in heraldry, has a lion's body and a man's head. He has three rows of voracious teeth and is sometimes shown with tusks, like a boar.

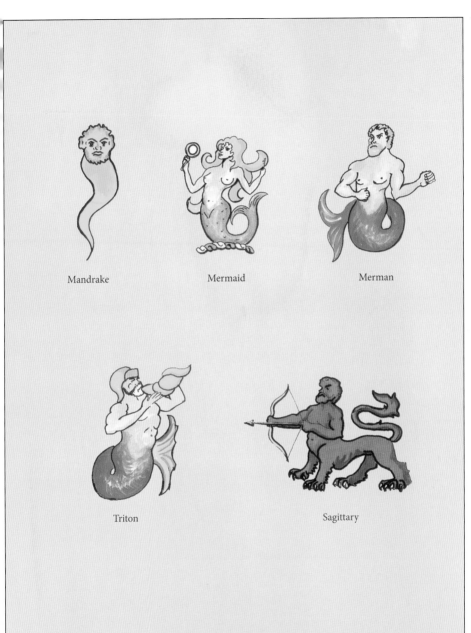

Mandrake

Mermaid

Merman

Triton

Sagittary

# CELESTIAL BEINGS

THE TERM "CELESTIAL BEINGS" COVERS A BROAD SPECTRUM IN HERALDRY, WITH EVERYTHING FROM CHERUBS AND SERAPHIMS TO PAGAN GODS AND ARCHANGELS REPRESENTED AS CHARGES. DESPITE THE DIVERSITY OF SUBJECTS, GODS AND ANGELS FIGURE RELATIVELY RARELY, AND DEPICTIONS OF CHRIST WERE LARGELY AVOIDED.

In heraldry it is more common to find allusion to heavenly beings by symbol rather than by direct representation. Examples do exist of Christ on the Cross, but very rarely, since it was widely felt to be improper to reduce so sacred a subject to heraldry. Though Inverness in Scotland bears "gules upon a cross the figure of Our Lord crucified proper," most of the very few representations of Christ, of his mother, or of the saints are found on the arms of ecclesiastical establishments. Some European towns display saints, but this is not a common practice.

Angels occasionally appear as supporters of coats of arms, both officially and unofficially, but again the practice is relatively—and perhaps, surprisingly—rare. In modern heraldry an angel is usually represented as a female figure, vested in a long robe, with wings, although depictions do vary somewhat from country to country. Historically angels belonged to a variety of different orders, each portrayed differently. Angel supporters are frequently used to display shields, as a decorative feature, when shown in churches.

Angels supporting a coat of arms on the facade of the Costa Palace, Piacenza, in Emilia-Romagna, Italy.

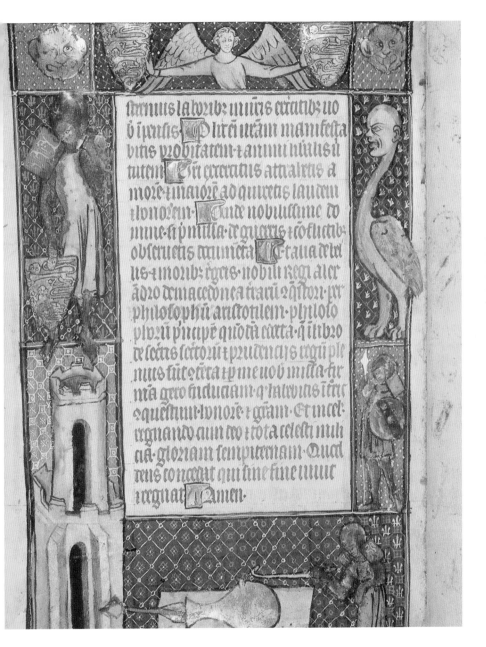

An illuminated canon (1326) from Christchurch, Oxford, showing an angel bearing the royal arms of England.

The coat of arms of the city of Budweis in the Czech Republic. An archangel stands guard over the city, bearing a sword and shield.

A crowned cupid stands elegantly upon a wreath of leaves, bearing arms across his naked body. The cupid is a timeless symbol of love and is always represented as a young boy with wings.

## ARCHANGELS IN HERALDRY

Archangels were definitely felt to be gentlemen in the medieval imagination and arms were attributed to them. The only one of great heraldic significance is St. Michael. He is usually depicted in armor, carrying out the fight against the devil, who is normally represented by a green dragon. St. Michael's arms were a red cross on a white field. He was evidently the model for the mythical St. George, who is now the patron saint of chivalry and also of England.

## HERALDIC CHERUBS

In heraldry, a cherub was generally only shown as the face of a boy, above a pair of wings. By representing the cherubim through infants' winged heads, the early heraldic painters meant them to be emblematic of a pure spirit glowing with love and intelligence. The head was viewed as the seat of the soul, and the wings denoted swiftness and spirit. The body or limbs of the cherub and seraph are seldom shown in heraldry, for what reason it is difficult to say—unless it be from the ambiguity of the descriptions in the sacred writings and the consequent difficulty of representing them. The heralds adopted the figure of speech termed "synecdoche," which adopts a part to represent the whole.

## OTHER CELESTIAL BEINGS

SERAPHIM He is shown as a man's face, with six wings, but only rarely.

CUPID A mythical rather than celestial being. The figure of Cupid does appear and is shown as a young boy, with wings and a bow and arrow.

MERCURY This god appears as a crest and charge and so do winged hands and feet. The Caducus, his serpent entwined staff, is also used as a charge.

APOLLO This god appears as the main charge of the arms of the Worshipful Company of Apothecaries. Apart from their use as supporters, representations of the whole human figure belong more to religious art and mythology than to heraldry.

The coat of arms of the town of Pisa in Italy, on Piazza dei Miracoli. Here, cherubs hold the town's crest aloft.

# HUMAN BEINGS

T HE WHOLE HUMAN FIGURE IS OFTEN
USED AS A SUPPORTER IN HERALDRY, IN
A VARIETY OF COSTUMES AND STYLES, BUT
IT IS MORE COMMON TO FIND ONLY PARTS
OF THE BODY USED AS CHARGES.

Heads, hands, legs, and hearts—either vested
or armored—all are used in heraldry in a wide
variety of ways. Parts of the human body can be
erased or couped in exactly the same way as the
parts of animal bodies.

## THE HUMAN HEAD
## IN HERALDRY

In most heraldic depictions of the human
head, it is shown in profile and is placed facing
dexter. It can be cut off at the neck or across the
shoulders, and the type—a maiden, a Saxon, a
Saracen, a Turk, and so on—should be specified
in the blazon. Any head can wear any kind of
crown or wreath.

Human heads are often used in heraldry
to recall conflicts of the past. The head of the
Saracen is particularly common, reflecting the
exploits of the crusader knights in the Holy
Land over a period of several hundred years.

Some families' coats of arms depict the
heads of defeated foes, such as the Scot's head
that features on the crest of the Hazelriggs
of Noseley in Leicestershire, England. The
appearance of this head commemorates the
family's part in the Scottish wars of Edward
III (1327–77). There are similar examples of
Englishmen's heads on various Welsh family
arms and vice-versa, although these were not
necessarily used as crests.

An illustration from Froizart's Chronicles, a 14th
century manuscript. The English army campaign in
France under the banner of St. George.

When complete human figures are depicted in heraldry—which is surprisingly rarely—they are normally shown as supporters of arms, as here. Heraldic emblems and coats of arms are often quite prosaic in theme and style when human figures are involved in the decoration. In this design on a church stained glass window, two honest- and earnest-looking women promote the legend "cleanliness is next to godliness."

# OTHER PARTS OF THE BODY

Various disembodied limbs and other human body parts frequently adorn heraldic designs.

**DEMI-FIGURE** This is a very common crest, and may be armored (in armor), habited (vested), or vested (dressed in).

**ARMS** These are often found as charges and crests. As crests they are usually found holding something in the hand. The blazon will sometimes say which arm it is. A "cubit arm" is one arm cut off cleanly below the elbow. "Embowed" means "bent at the shoulder," "Vambraced" means "in armor" and "Vested and cuffed" means "within a sleeve with a different colored cuff."

**HANDS** Hands are commonly used as a charge. The blazon will always say if right or left. "Apaumy" means "open, showing the palm" and "Closed" means "clenched or grasping an object."

**LEGS** Legs are found used in the same way. Whether they are cut off at, above, or below the knee will be stated in the blazon. Arms and legs can be placed either vertically ("palewise") erect or horizontally ("fesswise").

The crest of the Hamond-Graeme family, in which a skull is lifted by disembodied arms from atop a spike. This gruesome scene commemorates an ancestor's heroics at war, sometime in the 17th century.

This illustration shows a cubit arm (cut off cleanly below the elbow). It is described as vested because of the sleeve. In a blazon, vested and cuffed means that the cuff is of a different color from the sleeve.

Church funeral hatchments; the hatchment on the right shows "or three piles piercing a human heart gules." The heart is a common body part in heraldic art, as are the liver, the skull, and others.

# PLANETS AND STARS

THE GALAXY—AND PARTICULARLY THE SUN AND MOON—HELD A SPECIAL FASCINATION FOR THE HERALDIC ARTISTS OF CENTURIES PAST. JUST AS THE POSTURES OF ANIMALS, BIRDS, HUMANS, AND MYTHICAL BEASTS DENOTED SPECIAL SYMBOLISM, SO DID A VAST ARRAY OF STYLIZED SUNS, MOONS, STARS, AND PLANETS.

## THE CELESTIAL BODIES

As with just about everything else in heraldic design, the positions of the celestial bodies depicted as charges were very important. Equally, the various embellishments that were added to basic designs carried special significance. It is not always clear why a face was sometimes painted on a sun and sometimes not, but it certainly added to the desired effect in a design showing "the sun in splendor."

SUN  This is usually shown with numerous rays bursting out of the central body, sometimes accompanied by a face, sometimes not. "Sun burst" refers to the representation of a ray of sunlight from behind a cloud.

MOON  This is shown as a crescent. "Increscent" refers to a crescent moon facing the dexter; "Decrescent" refers to a crescent moon facing the sinister; "In her compliment" refers to the full moon shown with a face to avoid confusion with a plate.

STARS  A star is always called an "estoile" and is shown with six or more wavy rays.

RAINBOW  In heraldry, this is the representation of a half-ring divided into seven concentric narrow rings and arched upward, each end resting on a clump of clouds. To avoid the difficulty of finding seven different tinctures, the number of concentric rings is sometimes diminished to three, usually azure, or, and gules—that is, blue, gold, and red.

CLOUDS  These are usually seen with something issuing from them—perhaps sunrays or a human hand.

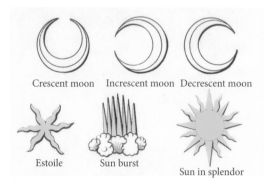

Crescent moon    Increscent moon    Decrescent moon

Estoile    Sun burst    Sun in splendor

A selection of heraldic depictions of the sun, moon, and stars.

Dramatic use of a sun on a sculptured coat of arms on a church in Emilia-Romagna, Italy.

For centuries the sun has been depicted "in splendor," often with a face—sometimes kind, sometimes cruel.

The ancient coat of arms of the Hungarian crown, (that of the Austro-Hungarian monarchy), featuring an increscent moon above a black eagle.

The coat of arms of Transylvania (again, belonging to the Austro-Hungarian monarchy), which forms part of the impaled coat of arms to the left.

# INANIMATE OBJECTS

THIS GROUP OF HERALDIC CHARGES ENCOMPASSES ALL KINDS OF ARTEFACTS, WEAPONS, TOOLS, BUILDINGS, SHIPS—REALLY EVERY KIND OF THING IMAGINABLE! IF IT COULD BE DRAWN, THE HERALDIC ARTISTS WOULD DRAW IT—NO MATTER HOW MUNDANE THE SUBJECT. IT IS BEYOND THE SCOPE OF THIS BOOK TO LIST ALL OBJECTS.

The main groups of inanimate objects featured in heraldry are outlined below. It is worth noting any obscurity or peculiarity in the terms used to describe the various charges.

## THE CROSS
By far the most important item among the inanimate objects is the cross. Because it is the symbol of Christianity and every Christian state took it as its emblem when it set out on the crusades, there is a bewildering variety of crosses. Some authorities list more than 150. Most of these are very rare; a dozen of the most common varieties are illustrated opposite.

## BUILDINGS
A wide range of these are used, but apart from the tower, the castle, and the bridge, most are rare. These appear as charges, crests, and badges. (The portcullis, a defensive gate, is also frequently seen).

## SHIPS
All kinds of ships have been used in heraldry and the type is usually specified. "Lymphand" is a galley (trading vessel) in full sail. (Anchors, fish traps, nets, fish spears, and tridents have also been used.)

## THE WEAPONS
Weapons of all kinds are commonly used throughout Europe and appear as charges, crests, and badges and are held or brandished by crests and supporters. The most common

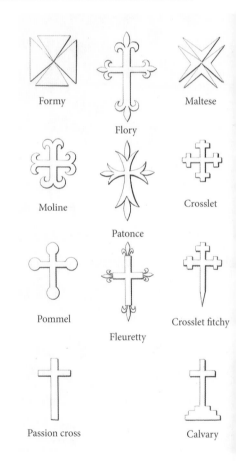

Formy

Flory

Maltese

Moline

Patonce

Crosslet

Pommel

Fleuretty

Crosslet fitchy

Passion cross

Calvary

Of the 150 or so different designs for the cross, some of the most common are illustrated here.

This stained-glass window of the armorial bearings of Sir Peter Tizard was created by Jane Gray.

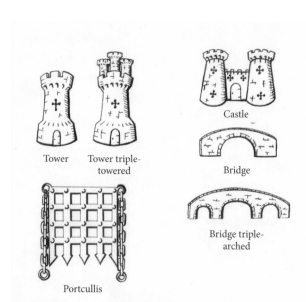

Tower

Tower triple-towered

Castle

Bridge

Bridge triple-arched

Portcullis

Illustrated here are the most commonly found buildings in heraldry.

The portcullis badge of Westminster on a roof boss of Westminster Abbey. This Tudor badge, the Duke of Westminster's badge, is now a common municipal symbol.

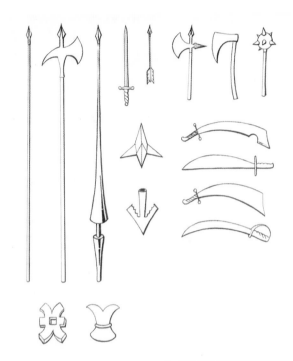

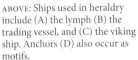

ABOVE: Ships used in heraldry include (A) the lymph (B) the trading vessel, and (C) the viking ship. Anchors (D) also occur as motifs.

ABOVE RIGHT: Illustrated here are various weapons used in heraldry.

RIGHT: Towers are shown in this stone carving of armorial bearings by S & I Winter.

are the sword, the seaaxe, the battleaxe, the arrow, the arrowhead, the peon, the caltrap, the spear, the tilting spear, the mace, and the coronel. The peon is a kind of broad arrowhead and the caltrap is a spiked object which was strewn on the ground to stop horses. The coronel was used to blunt the tip of a tilting spear.

## CLOTHING
All kinds of clothing—footwear, hats, armor, and gloves—are used as charges. Pilgrim staffs and bags are also seen. A "maunch" is a sleeve with pocket pendant.

## DOMESTIC ITEMS
Among the most commonly seen domestic items are cups, globes, chess rooks, books, buckles, keys, locks and fetterlocks, mill rinds, clarions, and bougets. There is more about these oddities in the following pages.

### MILL-RIND
This is the metal bracket which takes the spindle in the center of a millstone and holds a tie rod on the outside wall of a building.

### CLARION
This is a musical instrument, a kind of trumpet.

### BOUGET
This is a water carrier, consisting of two water buckets made of skin hanging from a yoke.

### FLEAM
This is a kind of surgical instrument, now obsolete.

## THE HERALDIC CROWNS
A variety of crowns are used as charges. They have nothing to do with rank, but serve to denote excellence in a sphere of activity. Note that these are termed crowns, not coronets. This is an important distinction in heraldry.

Many different forms of crowns are used as charges.

Anchors are a commonplace charge in many coats of arms with a maritime theme or association.

It is common to find a mix of different animals, liveries, and inanimate objects on heraldic shields. In the examples above, keys—a particularly ubiquitous choice of the heralds, offering obvious symbolism—are combined with rampant lions, crowns, and fleur-de-lis.

# ODDITIES

ALMOST EVERY TOOL AND ARTEFACT USED BY MAN HAS BEEN INCORPORATED INTO HERALDRY, AS WELL AS ITEMS OF CLOTHING OF EVERY KIND. SOME OF THESE MAY PRESENT DIFFICULTIES TO AN OBSERVER TRYING TO FORMULATE THE POSSIBLE BLAZON. A SELECTION OF THE MOST POPULAR UNUSUAL CHARGES IS PRESENTED HERE.

Indeed, with some modern examples it may be necessary to resort to the original Grant of Arms to ascertain what the charge is supposed to be. Here are a selection of items, used since ancient times, whose identity may not be readily apparent, but which will from time to time be encountered.

## MILL-RIND

This represents the metal plate used to reinforce the center of a millstone used for grinding flour from wheat. Devices of this kind are also found reinforcing buildings. They are seen outside the wall acting as plates for tie-rods that run through the house to prevent the walls from spreading outward. Nowadays they are often to be seen in the shape of an "S." They were sometimes cross-shaped and the crosses moline and recercle were often used.

## MAUNCH

This represents the sleeve of a medieval costume. These items were worn over an undergarment of some kind and were fastened to the bodice part of the garment by ribbands. It was presumably possible to do a mix-and-match of different colored maunches to the main part of the garment and even to each other. These sleeves had a long pocket hanging down from them.

## CHESS ROOK

The chess piece that we know as the pawn. It is drawn in this rather strange way to prevent confusion with the representation of a castle.

## CLARION

This is a kind of wind instrument, not to be confused with the pan pipes, that also appear.

## BOUGET

This device should be thought of as a yoke to go over the shoulders, and hung from it two buckets made from animal skin. These were used for carrying water. When armies had to be moved long distances by foot, obviously the provision of water for man and beast was a constant and serious problem.

## FLEAM

This charge is used to represent the small instrument that surgeons used to open the vein in the medical practice of blood letting. Apparently it was thought that the symptoms of fever might be relieved through draining blood to reduce the pressure in the patient's body.

## SCYTHE

This long-handled instrument was, and still is, used to mow grass and other herbaceous growth and has been included here to make the point that it should not be confused with a fleam.

## WOOLSACK

In the Middle Ages the wealth of England came from wool. The shorn fleeces were packed and then sewn into large sacks, shown with a tottle at each corner, so that they could be picked up. They were a symbol of wealth. They should not be confused with a cushion shown with a

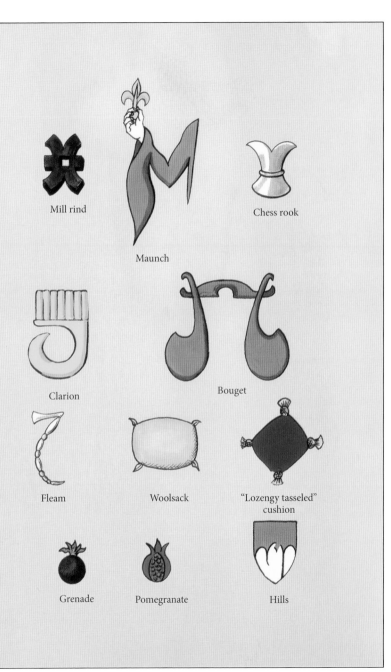

Mill rind

Maunch

Chess rook

Clarion

Bouget

Fleam

Woolsack

"Lozengy tasseled"
cushion

Grenade

Pomegranate

Hills

tassel at each corner, though this is often shown "lozengy tasseled."

## GRENADE AND POMEGRANATE

The grenade is shown as a round ball with flames coming out of the top. The pomegranate is usually shown as a round fruit, leafed at the top, but split open in order to reveal the many red seeds inside. It is important not to confuse the two items. The grenade is usually black and the pomegranate green.

## HILLS

This is obvious when you know what it is supposed to be, but initially it can look a little puzzling. It is quite often found in Italian and papal heraldry.

## ICEBERG

This uncommon charge is blazoned "an iceberg proper."

## BEACON

In this basket a fire was lit as a warning or signal and was visible from a long way off. Beacons were used as lights for navigation, as lighthouses before they existed, to warn of approaching danger or as celebration. As long as each beacon was in sight of the next, news could be spread very quickly.

## GRID IRON

An iron placed on a fire upon which to stand pots or lay meat for grilling. The common use of barbecues has made this item familiar to us once more.

## PASSION NAILS

These are supposed to represent the nails with which Jesus was nailed to the cross.

## BATTERING RAM

In the days when defenders had the annoying habit of locking themselves inside fortified buildings, attackers had to resort to this instrument, wielded by as many men as were needed to lift it, to break down the door. Large ones were even constructed out of whole tree trunks and suspended on ropes in a wheeled cart, including a roof to protect those within from the missiles of those without. Today, small two-person versions of these are sometimes used by the police to break down doors.

## COOKING POT

Used particularly in Spanish heraldry and allusive to the right and power of raising an army. This was only allowed to certain grandees and so its use was allusive of importance.

## SPUR AND FETLOCK

The spur can still be seen today on ceremonial uniforms, but at one time it was commonly used by horsemen to urge their mounts to greater speed or more effort. It was worn strapped to the heel of the boot. The fetlock was used to fasten the two legs of a captive or beast together. One fetlock was placed on each leg and they were chained or tied together.

## CORONAL OR CORONEL

This item was placed over the point of a lance when jousting to prevent injury to the opponent. It should not be confused with a chess rook.

## PURSE

This item occasionally appears in different guises. As a pilgrim's purse it is usually shown with a staff. The great seals of a sovereign were kept in a purse and its use might indicate a person of high office.

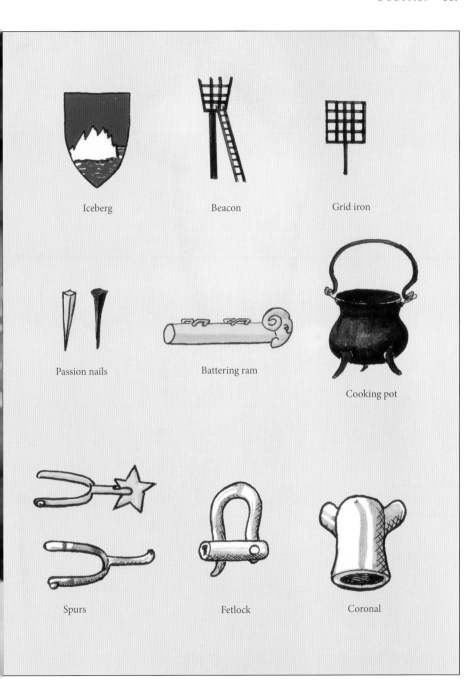

Iceberg

Beacon

Grid iron

Passion nails

Battering ram

Cooking pot

Spurs

Fetlock

Coronal

# SPORTS AND GAMES

S PORTS AND GAMES WERE HUGELY IMPORTANT IN MEDIEVAL LIFE, NOT ONLY AS FORMS
OF RECREATION BUT ALSO AS PRACTICE FOR THE WARS THAT FREQUENTLY OCCURRED.
ARCHERY AND JOUSTING WERE PARTICULARLY SIGNIFICANT IN THIS REGARD, AND THERE
WAS NOTHING MORE SYMBOLIC IN HERALDIC LIFE THAN THE TOURNAMENT.

## HERALDS AND TOURNAMENTS

Owing to their knowledge of armorial bearings, heralds were required to recognize and announce contestants at tournaments and it became their responsibility to organize and referee these events. Because of the social nature of the events and the desire by everyone to put on a good display, heralds were necessary to advise would-be contestants about the choice of armorial bearings that they could use. They were able to make sure that no one chose the arms of another already in use. People came to them for advice on heraldic matters and they began to keep lists of all the armorial bearings used at different tournaments, gatherings, and battles and of the people who bore them. These lists were collected on long rolls of parchment and were called Rolls of Arms, or simply Rolls. Many of these have survived and they provide a valuable record of early heraldry.

## SPORTS AND GAMES AS SYMBOLS

As well as being central to the business of heraldry itself, sports and games became increasingly important charges and symbols on crests and coats of arms throughout the Middle Ages. Sometimes these verged on the light-hearted, in keeping with the recreational aspects of many games, as opposed to the warfaring practice that many sports represented. For example, the Tosetti family of Massiola, in northern Italy, contrived a family coat of arms featuring two tennis-playing youths, who, for unexplained reasons, are completely naked.

Elsewhere, indoor games came to be featured on family arms. Chess pieces were particularly popular, and backgammon boards were part of the design of the Pegrez family of England. Meanwhile in Wales, the Lamphrey family of Pembrokeshire chose to decorate their heraldic shield with images of dice, carefully arranged in coded groups across the arms.

A modern take on knight chess pieces on a heraldic crest. Pieces from chess and other board games such as backgammon make regular appearances on many families' coats of arms.

One of the most dramatic and symbolic of all events associated with heraldry was the medieval tournament. In this modern re-creation of a contest, two would-be knights engage in remarkably authentic-looking jousting.

These two knights, dressed in their full chivalric regalia, prepare to do combat at a tournament. This was a great opportunity not only to show competence with sword and lance but also to put on the best display of their personal heraldic coats of arms.

# CANTING OR ALLUSIVE ARMS

CANTING, ALLUSIVE, OR PUNNING ARMS PERTAIN TO THOSE MANY EXAMPLES OF HERALDIC DESIGNS THAT HAVE BEEN DEVISED AS A PLAY ON THE BEARER'S NAME. THIS APPEALING FORM OF HERALDRY HAS BEEN IMMENSELY POPULAR FOR CENTURIES AND CAN ACCOUNT FOR MORE THAN HALF THE DESIGNS FOUND IN SOME COUNTRIES.

It would be very nice to be able to look at a coat of arms and ascertain its meaning and the reason why those particular charges have been chosen and then determine exactly what they are saying. However, in most instances this is not possible, as the rationale behind the composition of the achievement is not known. In canting or punning arms, there is an obvious connection and it is possible to understand the reason behind the choice of subject. Here is a selection of well known allusive arms from around the world of heraldry, illustrated with some classic examples of the form.

LORD FISHER OF LAMBETH has a crest of a kingfisher proper, holding in its dexter claw a fleur-de-lys sable.

LORD GEDDES has geds (pike) as charges, supporters, and on his crest.

BAYNES bears sable a shin bone in fess surmounted by another in page argent.

BULL displays sable three astronomical signs of Taurus, or.

BUTLER bears covered cups.

COOT bears argent a chevron sable between three coots, close (wings by their sides) proper.

CORBET bears or a raven (known as a corbie) sable.

METCALF bears argent three calves sable.

VEAL bears two lightning strikes in chevron between three calves.

SWINTON bears boars as charges, supporters, and crest.

SHAKESPEAR bears or on a bend sable a tilting spear or.

SHEARER bears reaping hooks.

LILLY bears gules, three lilies slipped argent.

APPLEGARTH bears three apples slipped gules.

ARUNDEL bears sable six swallows (hirondels) argent.

ASPEN bears azure an aspen leaf or.

ALPE OF NORFOLK azure a fess ermine between three alpes (bullfinches) argent.

THE TOWN OF BERN bears gules a bear sable.

THE COUNTS OF BAR bear azure crusily (strewn with crosses) two barbels haurient, and adorsed or.

BEAN bears gules three bean pods pendant or.

BAT bears or three bats sable.

n "canting" or punning heraldry, the direct association between the image and the name of the bearer is key. The thoroughly obvious connection between the name of the Swiss town of Bern and the large black bear that bestrides its coat of arms is a perfect example of this heraldic form.

The coat of arms of the dauphin of France, featuring two dolphins.

BROCKET has as a crest a brocket (a young stag) lodged sable.

BROCK OF KENT has on a mount vert a badger sable.

THE FATHER OF ANN BOLEYN bore argent a chevron gules between three bulls heads sable armed or, though Ann Boleyn was granted a shield of six quarters by Henry VIII which did not include this coat.

THE KINGDOM OF CASTILE in Spain bore gules a three towered castle or.

The neighboring KINGDOM OF LEON bore argent a lion rampant purple.

COLUMBALL bore sable three doves argent beaked and membered gules, in their beaks sprigs of olive proper ("columb" means dove in Latin).

DE LA HAY bears argent the sun in splendor or.

THE DAUPHIN, the heir to the French throne, bore azure a dolphin embowed or allusive to his Dukedom, from the Celtic *dalnapen*

which means "district of the chief" and became corrupted to Dauphin.

ELMS bears ermine on a bend sable, ten elm leaves or. Faisant bears azure three pheasants or, beaked and membered gules.

FIGURA OF SPAIN bears or five fig leaves in saltyre vert.

GRICE bore quarterly, gules and azure on a bend ermine, three boars passant, sable armed or. (A young boar is known as a "grice.")

This gives some idea of the variety of items encountered: Herringhams bear herrings; Roach bear roaches; Lucy bears lucies (pike); Mills bear mill-rinds and Moore bears moorcocks. Pont bears a bridge of two arches; de Pines has three gold pine cones and Tremaynes bears three arms joined at the shoulder. Whalley bears whales.

If you know the name of the bearer, you can deduce the reason for the charge, but you cannot look at a shield and deduce from it the name of the bearer, for there may be many different reasons why those charges have been given to that person and they may have nothing to do with his name.

The heraldic shield of the Grice family, featuring three young boars, known as "grice."

This is the proud and historic coat of arms of the province of Leon and Castile in Spain, in which once again the link between name and imagery is unassailable.

# CHAPTER 5

# HISTORICAL
# CASE STUDIES

# THE ROYAL ARMS OF ENGLAND

I T HAS BECOME THE PRACTICE TO DISPLAY MANY DIFFERENT COATS OF ARMS ON
ONE SHIELD AND, ONCE THIS IS PROPERLY UNDERSTOOD, MUCH MORE SENSE CAN BE
MADE OF THE APPARENT CONFUSION. A GOOD CASE IN POINT IS THE ROYAL ARMS OF
ENGLAND AND THE UNITED KINGDOM, WHICH HAVE EVOLVED OVER THE CENTURIES.

## MANY COATS OF ARMS
## ON ONE SHIELD

As we have seen in the section on marshaling
of arms (pages 124–39), the main reason for
combining many coats of arms on one shield
is to demonstrate, in the case of royal arms,
sovereignty over different lands. In the case
of personal arms, it is to show that the wearer
represents families other than his own, that
have become joined to his through marriage
and who have no one in the male line to
represent them.

## THE ROYAL ARMS
## OF ENGLAND

The display of royal arms changes with the
dynastic fortunes of a sovereign. A judicious
marriage with an heiress would bring more
territory under his control and this would be
demonstrated by displaying his spouse's coat of
arms with his own, so that they are inherited
by the heir. The arms of the United Kingdom,
in their present form, have evolved over the
years from the Royal Arms of England in the
following way.

The arms being gules (red) two lions passant
guardant or (gold) have become accepted as
the arms of the Duchy of Normandy and have
been assigned to the Norman Kings of England.
In 1152 Henry II married Eleanor, daughter of
the Duke of Aquitaine and that territory came
under English rule. Her arms were gules (red)
a lion passant guardant or (gold). It is thought
that this lion was added to the coat of arms

of Normandy and the coat, gules three lions
passant guardant or was produced. This device,
which became known simply as "England" has
remained the heraldic emblem of that country
ever since, even though the lands of Aquitaine
in France, were subsequently lost.

## UNION AND DISUNITY
## WITH FRANCE

In 1308 Edward II of England married Isabella,
the only daughter of the King of France.
Although she had three brothers, none of them
produced an heir and so her son, Edward III
of England, claimed the throne of France as
rightful heir, and in 1340 placed the gold lilies
on a blue field of France in the first and third
quarters of his arms to reinforce this claim.
The French, however, subscribing to Salic law,
decided that the crown could not descend
through a woman and chose instead his second
cousin, Philip, Count of Valois to be their king.
However, England continued to display this
claim until it was finally dropped in 1801.

Henry IV of England followed the practice
of Charles V of France and reduced the number
of the fleurs-de-lys to three.

Henry V of England restarted the wars
against France and was victorious at the famous
Battle of Agincourt in 1415. In 1420 he married
Katherine, daughter of Charles VI, the French
king. In 1422 he was on his way to be crowned
King of France, when he fell ill and died.
The arms of England remained unchanged
throughout the dynastic and disastrous Wars of

Arms of France

Arms of Scotland

Arms of England

Arms of James I
of England,
VI of Scotland

Arms of
Edward III

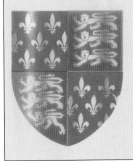

the Roses, when so many of England's nobles and princes were either killed, executed, or died in other ways. The Tudors eventually succeeded the Plantagenets as the sovereigns of England following the Battle of Bosworth. When Elizabeth I died childless in 1603, the crown passed to her nearest relative, James Stewart, King of Scotland. He became James VI of Scotland and James I of England. Thus the two kingdoms became joined and the arms were altered accordingly. Even though the last piece of French territory had been lost during the reign of Mary I, the claim to the French crown was still maintained and the arms became England and France quartered together in the first and fourth grand quarters, Scotland in the second and Ireland in the third.

## CIVIL WAR AND STRIFE

James I was succeeded by his son, Charles I. These were, however, troubled times and the royal prerogative and authority was being challenged by a parliament of the people flexing their muscles. Following a bitter civil war, the king was executed and a Commonwealth was established, which lasted for eleven years. During this time the royal arms were suspended and a display of arms for the Commonwealth was devised displaying on a shield the Cross of St. George, the saltyre of St. Andrew, and the harp of Ireland, over all of which was placed an escutcheon of the arms of Oliver Cromwell (the leader of the Commonwealth).

In 1660 the monarchy was reinstated and Charles II, son of the executed Charles I, was crowned. The Commonwealth came to an end and the Royal Arms were restored. In 1662 Charles II married Katherine, daughter of John IV of Portugal, but died childless and so was succeeded by his brother, James II.

James, by his first wife, Anne Hyde, daughter of the Earl of Clarenden, had two daughters. The elder, Mary, married William III, Prince of Orange; he was the son of James II's sister Mary, who had married William

II, Prince of Orange in 1641. James II was an unpopular and unsuccessful king and in 1688 William III of Orange was persuaded to invade England and raise a successful rebellion against his uncle. The king fled and in 1689 William and his wife Mary were proclaimed joint sovereigns. As William was an elected king, he placed his paternal arms of Nassau, azure (blue) billety (scattered with small billets) a lion rampant or (gold) on an escutcheon (small shield) upon the arms of England. Because his wife was also queen in her own right, they displayed her arms (those of her father) with his, side by side on the same shield.

## MORE HERALDIC CHANGES

William outlived his queen and when he died childless in 1702 he was succeeded (by Act of Parliament) by his wife's younger sister Anne. James II's son by his second wife, Mary of Modena, being brought up a Catholic by his mother, was debarred from succession by the Protestant English parliament. The escutcheon of Nassau was removed from the Royal Arms. In 1707 Scotland became united with England and the arms were again altered to show in the first and fourth grand quarter, England impaling Scotland (that is placed together side by side) France second and Ireland third quarter.

Since the Commonwealth, the English Parliament had gained considerably in power, and when Queen Anne died in 1714 they sought to succeed her with her nearest Protestant relative, ignoring the many who had a better genealogical claim to the throne, but who were Catholic. The crown was offered to George, the Elector of Hanover, grandson of Elizabeth, sister of Charles I.

George I was crowned king of England in 1714 and thus began the reign of the Hanoverian House of Guelph. The Royal Arms were changed by replacing in the fourth grand quarter the impaled arms of England and Scotland with the arms of Hanover. These are in three quarters, tierced in pairle reversed (the disposition of the quarters,

The magnificent display of the banners of the present Knights
of Bath, in the Henry VII chapel of Westminster Abbey.

Westminster Abbey in London is the home of many of the greatest English and royal heraldic designs and charges. This is the ancient tomb of the Countess of Hertford.

see on to Division of the Field) first gules (red) two lions passant guardant or (gold)—Brunswick; second or (gold) seme (scattered over with) hearts gules (red) a lion rampant azure (blue)—Luneburg; third gules (red) a horse courant (galloping) argent (white)—Westphalia; overall, an escutcheon gules charged with the crown of Charlemagne or (gold)—the badge of Arch Treasurer of the Holy Roman Empire.

In 1801, in the reign of George III, following the union with Ireland, the arms were once again remarshaled and became first and fourth England; second Scotland; third Ireland. The pretention to the kingdom of France was finally dropped. Overall was placed an escutcheon of Hanover with a representation of the Elector's cap placed above it. In 1816, when Hanover became a kingdom, this was changed to a royal crown.

In 1837 Victoria became Queen of England, but because of Salic laws she could not become Queen of Hanover. This office passed to her uncle, Ernest. The escutcheon of Hanover was removed from the British royal arms and they took the form that is still in use today.

This is how the Royal Coat of Arms of England and the United Kingdom appears today.

# THE ACHIEVEMENT OF ARMS OF PHILIP II OF SPAIN AND MARY I OF ENGLAND

ANOTHER GOOD EXAMPLE OF SEVERAL DIFFERENT COATS OF ARMS BEING DISPLAYED TOGETHER ON THE SAME SHIELD IS THAT CREATED BY THE MARRIAGE OF PHILIP II OF SPAIN TO MARY I OF ENGLAND. IT SHOWS THE SOVEREIGNTY OF A LARGE PART OF EUROPE ASSEMBLED INTO THE HANDS OF ONE PERSON, BY FORTUITOUS DYNASTIC MARRIAGES.

Philip was a Hapsburg and called himself King of Spain, King of Sicily, Duke of Burgundy, Archduke of Austria, and Count of Hapsburg, Flanders, and the Tyrol.

Philip II's forebears were the Archdukes of Austria and had acquired the rich dukedoms of Burgundy, Brabant, and Flanders by marriage.

In 1347 Louis II Count of Flanders married Margaret heiress of John II, Duke of Brabant. In 1356 their daughter married Philip I, Duke of Burgundy. He died in 1361 without an heir and the vacant dukedom was given by King John II of France to his son Philip, who became known as Philip the Bold of Burgundy. In 1369 he

Philip II of Spain.

Mary I of England.

Arms of John II,
Duke of Brabant

Arms of King
Alphonso IX of Leon

Arms of Ferdinand III, King
of Castile and Leon

Arms of Peter III, King
of Aragon

Arms of Manfred,
King of Sicily

Arms of Frederick, King
of Sicily

Arms of John,
King of Aragon

Arms of Granada

Arms of Joanna the Mad,
Heiress of Spain

Arms of Philip I, King
of Spain and Sicily

Arms of Charles I, King of
Spain, Archduke of Austria,
Duke of Burgundy

married the widow Margaret, former wife of the previous duke. His great grandson, Charles the Bold, was killed in 1477 leaving only a daughter, Margaret, as the most eligible heiress in Europe. That same year she married Maximillian, Archduke of Austria and Holy Roman Emperor. Their son, Philip, Archduke of Austria and Duke of Burgundy, married Joanna the Mad, daughter of Ferdinand, King of Aragon, and Isabella, Queen of Castile. Spain had been five separate kingdoms that had become united over the passage of time.

## BACKGROUND TO UNITY

In 1198 Alphonso IX King of Leon had married Berengaria, heiress of Alphonso VIII of Castile and their son Ferdinand III became King of both kingdoms in 1230 when his father died.

In 1282 Peter III, King of Aragon married Constance daughter of Manfred, King of Sicily. They produced two sons, James the elder inherited the senior Kingdom of Aragon, and Frederick, the younger, the junior Kingdom of Sicily. Frederick displayed both his father's arms and those of his mother on his shield quartered, in saltyre (that is, he divided the shield into four sections, diagonally, and placed his paternal arms in the top and bottom sections and his mother's in the two side sections). Divisions of a shield such as this are called quarterings, be there two or two hundred.

In 1409, Frederick's line having ended, the Crown of Sicily was offered to Martin I, King of Aragon which he accepted to become Martin II of Sicily, unusually succeeding his son, Martin I. Thus the two kingdoms became united and Martin displayed the arms Aragon and Sicily impaled, that is put together on one shield, side by side.

In 1420 John, King of Aragon, married Blanche, Queen of Navarra, and displayed a quartered coat of the arms of Aragon and Navarra to signify the union.

In 1479 Ferdinand, King of Aragon (Navarra and Sicily) married Isabella Queen of Castile and Leon. They displayed arms of Castile and Leon quartered in the first and fourth grand quarters (a quarter that is itself quartered is called a "grand quarter") with Aragon and Sicily impaled in the second and third quarters. In 1494 the Kingdom of Granada was recaptured from the Moors and the pomegranate emblem of this kingdom was added to the display of arms as a quartering in point, pointed.

## SPANISH UNION

The daughter of Ferdinand and Isabella, Joanna the Mad, therefore inherited the whole of Spain, and in 1494 she married Philip, Duke of Burgundy.

In 1504 Queen Isabella died and Philip became Philip I, King of Spain and Sicily. His son, Charles, was in time also appointed Holy Roman Emperor.

However, when Charles died this title passed to his brother, Ferdinand, who had married Anne, heiress of Bohemia and Hungary. Charles' son was Philip II, King of Spain, King of Sicily, Archduke of Austria, Duke of Burgundy, and Count of Hapsburg, Flanders, and Tyrol. In 1554, he married Mary I, Queen of England. He had hoped to tuck the gold lions of England and the fleur-de-lys of France that Mary displayed on her arms as further quarterings in his own achievement (a display of arms of any kind is called an achievement) but this was frustrated by the obstinacy of the British people. They were worried that their queen would marry an erstwhile enemy—and a Catholic to boot. Mary, who was the daughter of Catherine of Aragon, had been brought up a Catholic, and when she became queen she attempted to bring the country back to the true faith. Unfortunately she tried to use the same bloody methods that her brother had used in suppressing it. It was obvious that she should turn to her cousin Philip to help her. He was later to lead an expedition against her Protestant sister, Elizabeth. Her mother Catherine of Aragon had been the sister of Joanna the Mad, Philip's grandmother. However, the English people were very much against Philip calling himself King

"Bloody Mary" tried to reinstate Catholicism in England using the most barbaric of methods. The Catholic King Philip of Spain was her cousin and ally, and ultimately her husband, in a marriage with extraordinary dynastic ramifications, the least of which was a highly complex achievement of arms.

of England, and resistance was so great that he could only declare a dual monarchy. Mary and Philip were each sovereign of their own land and Philip could only place the English arms beside his own, in impalement. The marriage was not a success and he eventually returned to Spain, abandoning both his wife and any idea of acquiring England.

Mary died in 1558 and in 1560 Philip of Spain married Elizabeth, daughter of Henry II, King of France. He was disappointed too, in that he was never elected Holy Roman Emperor, although he did acquire the crown of Portugal in 1580 when John III died, for he had married that king's daughter as his first wife, and he subsequently added the arms of Portugal on an escutcheon to his achievement.

Thus, a complicated sequence of events resulted in a quite astonishing achievement of arms—at least for the duration of the marriage.

The achievement of arms formed by the marriage of Philip II of Spain and Mary I of England.

# THE ACHIEVEMENT OF ARMS OF VISCOUNT LORD SAVAGE AND HIS WIFE ELIZABETH

THE ACHIEVEMENT OF ARMS OF VISCOUNT LORD SAVAGE AND HIS WIFE ELIZABETH, DAUGHTER OF LORD THOMAS D'ARCY, IS AN EXAMPLE OF TWO MANY-QUARTERED COATS OF ARMS DISPLAYED TOGETHER ON A SHIELD, SIDE BY SIDE. THIS IS TO SAY THAT THE COATS OF ARMS ARE "IMPALED."

In England an impalement of arms such as this only lasts for the lifetime of the marriage. Any heirs of the marriage do not continue to display the arms of their mother in this way, because her paternal arms would be carried into the next generation by her brothers. Arms only become permanently attached to others when they belong to a woman who has no brothers to carry her paternal arms onward and so she, in fact, becomes the heraldic heiress of her father. If there is more than one daughter they become equal heiresses and any quarterings that they have can be added to the paternal achievement by their heirs, to descend permanently through the family.

## UNDERSTANDING THE ACHIEVEMENT

The first thing to be noticed from the Savage coat is that there is an uneven pattern of quarters—there are more in one half than the other. This should alert you to the fact that this is an impalement. As you look at the shield you will discern that in the top left corner (as you look at it), the first quarter is argent (white) six lioncels (little lions) sable (black). This coat is again repeated in the bottom right-hand corner of the middle (as you look at it). Similarly, if you look at the right-hand half of the shield (as you look at it), you will see that a coat argent (white)

three cinquefoils (five-petaled flowers) gules (red) are similarly repeated. This confirms that this is an impalement—the arms of two people placed together on the same shield. In this case both paternal arms are repeated. This is only done if there is an empty quarter.

## IDENTIFYING THE BEARERS OF ARMS

In the case of this achievement the bearers are known. However, if this were not the case, reference books called "Ordinaries of Arms" might help. There is a correct way of describing the design of a coat of arms and such a description in the right order and using the right terms is called a "blazon." Provided that you can arrive at the correct blazon for each of the coats, you could look them up in an Ordinary of Arms. However, though this will tell you to which family each of these coats belongs, only a great deal of patient genealogical research will tell you how they came to be incorporated in this actual achievement. Fortunately, although there are achievements with more quarterings than this in existence, you are far more likely to come across shields displaying a much less daunting array.

It is interesting to note that, despite the best efforts of the parties to unite their arms, the impalement would not last indefinitely.

This achievement of arms shows the impaled bearings of Thomas, Viscount Savage,
together with those of his wife Elizabeth, co-heiress of Lord Thomas D'Arcy.

# APPENDIX:

# HERALDRY TODAY

I T IS THE SHEER DIVERSITY AND FLEXIBILITY OF HERALDRY THAT HAS ENSURED THE SURVIVAL OF THIS UNIQUE ART FORM UP TO THE PRESENT DAY. THEREFORE, IT SEEMS FITTING TO END THIS BOOK AS IT BEGAN—BY CELEBRATING THE MODERN RELEVANCE AND USAGE OF POSSIBLY THE GREATEST MEDIEVAL LEGACY IN SOCIETY.

The variety of ways in which heraldic bearings can be displayed, their decorative function and intriguing rules of form, have meant that this most singular of arts and social sciences remains entirely relevant today. The ownership of a coat of arms—whether it be one long in the family or one newly granted—is a matter of justifiable pride, a pride that can be expressed by displaying and using the arms in a wide variety of ways. Provided that they are employed with good taste, their use can only enhance the appearance of personal items and artefacts.

Artists and craftsmen and some creative agencies specialize in supplying work of an heraldic nature. Having said that, it is very important, when commissioning heraldic work, to make sure that the artist is a competent exponent of the form who will render the work both artistically and correctly. Heraldry is not a representational art. The task of the heraldic artist is to convey a brief message by using symbols. It is the symbolism of the items that he or she is trying to portray, not the actual item, that is of utmost importance. He or she has to work with full regard to historical precedent and style, without forgetting that he or she is an artist of his or her own time. It is worth going to a specialist agency which will be eager to meet both these ends and which will have on hand competent craftspeople who can undertake work in all kinds of media.

ON CHINA  Painted and fired armorial painting and decoration.

ON CLOTH  Painted, printed, and sewn flags, banners, and standards. Embroidered fire screens, stool and seat covers, chair backs. Painted and printed bedspreads. Sewn spinnaker sails for yachts. Heraldic costumes.

ON GLASS  Engraved on table glass, doors and windows, table tops, and firescreens. Stained-glass windows and hanging plaques.

ON JEWELRY  Engraved rings, seals, personal items. Cast sculptured items, car mascots. Enameled and jeweled cuff links, badges, and brooches. Enameled box lids and wall plaques.

ON LEATHER  Embossed and gilded book bindings and covers, desk sets, and chairbacks, boxes, and belts.

ON PAPER AND VELLUM  Paintings of heraldic achievements, illuminated and calligraphic illustrations, family trees, book plates in black and white and in full color.

ON WOOD  Wall plaques, carved, and gilded or painted. Carved newel posts, carved, painted and gilded backs and panels on furniture. Carved and painted or gilded shields.

As we have seen, not all heraldry is entirely serious in intent—there is a long tradition of "punning" or "canting" in this art form. This continues to this day. In the unusual and humorous design above, prepared by a specialist heraldic artist for a Russian client, the arms combine a grenade, a pomegranate, and a dragon in crest. With the advantages of modern technology, today this design could be replicated on any number of different media.

# GLOSSARY

ERALDIC LANGUAGE IS CONSIDERED TO BE DIFFICULT TO UNDERSTAND BY SOME PEOPLE, PROBABLY BECAUSE SO MUCH OF IT IS DERIVED FROM MEDIEVAL FRENCH. HOWEVER, IT IS ACTUALLY QUITE EASY TO COMPREHEND ONCE YOU HAVE MASTERED SOME BASIC TERMS AND EXPRESSIONS. THE KEY ONES ARE EXPLAINED HERE.

**ACHIEVEMENT OF ARMS** The complete assemblage of heraldic accessories assigned to an individual, corporation, or state.

**ADDORSED** Of beasts or charges, back-to-back.

**AFFRONTY** Of a charge, facing the observer.

**ANGLED** Of a line of partition, set at an angle.

**APAUMY** Of a hand or gauntlet, open to show the palm.

**ARCH (ARCHY)** Of a line of partition, in the form of an arch.

**ARGENT** The color silver or white, a tincture of heraldry; a metal.

**ARMED** Of a human being or limb clothed in armor; the claws, beak, horns, or tusks of a creature, in a separate, specified color.

**ARMET** A totally enclosed, close-fitting helmet with opening front.

**ARMIGER** A person entitled to bear arms.

**ARMORIAL** A book listing armorial bearings alphabetically by the names of the bearers.

**ARMORIAL BEARINGS** The symbols born by an armiger—his coat armor, shield, and banner to distinguish him from others.

**ATTRIBUTED ARMS** Armorial bearings given to people who existed before heraldry and to celestial and legendary figures.

**AUGMENTATION** An additional charge or device awarded to an armiger as a reward for merit in some field or to commemorate a special event.

**AZURE** The color blue, a tincture of heraldry.

**BADGE** An heraldic device belonging to an armiger, worn by his retainers and sympathizers.

**BANNER** A square or rectangular flag upon which armorial bearings are displayed.

**BAR** A narrow strip on the shield in a horizontal plane ("barry," with several such strips).

**BARS GEMEL** Horizontal bars, arranged in pairs.

**BASILISK** An heraldic monster, a reptile said to be hatched by a serpent from a cock's egg.

**BATH, KNIGHTS OF THE** Active order of knights in Great Britain, in civil and military divisions.

**BATTLED (EMBATTLED)** Of a line of partition, having a crenelated edge like a battlement.

**BATON** A narrow, diagonal band not reaching the edge of the shield, in England sometimes in the form of the baton sinister, a mark of illegitimacy.

**BEAKED** Of a beak, in a separate specified color.

**BELLED** With bells, attached to a hawk's leg for hawking, in a separate specified color.

**BEND** A diagonal strip on the shield from sinister to dexter top; an ordinary "per bend," divided in the same plane; "In bend," charges placed in this plane.

**BEND SINISTER** A diagonal strip on the shield from dexter to sinister top.

**BENDLET** A narrow bend.

**BENDY** Covered with an even number of bends.

**BEVELED** Of a line of partition, broken so as to have two equally acute, alternate angles.

**BEZANT (BYZANT)** A gold roundel representing a coin.

**BEZANTY** Covered with gold coins.

**BICORPORATE** Two bodies joined to one head.

**BILLET** A rectangular shape, placed on end, representing a block of wood, usually used in large numbers to cover a field.

**BILLETY** Covered with billets.

**BLAZON** The written description of armorial

bearings—to "blazon" is to describe armorial bearings in words.

BORDURE A narrow band around the edge of the shield.

CABOSHED Of a head, front-facing, and cut off behind the ears.

CANTING Armorial bearings that in their concept and design include some reference or allusion to the name of the bearer.

CANTON A square section, smaller than a quartering in the top dexter or sinister corner of the shield; a sub-ordinary.

CENTAUR A monster, half man and half horse.

CHAPEAU A hat with a turned-up lining of fur, placed over the helm on which the crest stands; symbolic of especial dignity.

CHARGE Any device placed upon a shield or upon another item.

CHEVRON A V-shaped strip, inverted, an ordinary ("Per chevron," the field or any area of color divided as by a chevron).

CHEVRONELS A bent bar on an escutcheon, half the breadth of the chevron; a small chevron.

CHIEF The top section of the shield; an ordinary; ("in chief," of charges placed in this area on a shield).

CINQUEFOIL A stylized flower, with five petals.

CIRCLET A riband placed around a shield bearing a motto, usually of one of the orders of knighthood.

COAT OF ARMS A synonymous term for coat armor; now come to mean that which was painted on the coat, the armorial bearings. Because these are nowadays shown on a shield, a shield with armorial bearings painted on it is known as a coat of arms.

COLLEGE OF ARMS The building in London where English heralds have their chambers.

COMPARTMENT A representation of the ground or whatever on which the supporters, shield, and motto stand.

CORONET A metal, decorated headwear, symbolic of rank.

COUNTER Opposite.

COUPED Of anything, cut off cleanly, for example an arm, head, or branch.

CREST A decorative accessory placed on the helmet.

CROWN (HERALDIC) A symbolic charge used to denote an interest in a particular activity

CROZIER A ceremonial staff, symbolizing the role of a shepherd, used by a bishop.

DANCY Of a line of partition, toothed or indented.

DEVICE An artistic, traditional, or heraldic symbol (or symbols) chosen to represent a person.

DEXTER Right, considered from the point of view of the person bearing the shield, thus standing behind it.

DIAPERING A pattern in tone, on a plain field, to represent brocade; sometimes worked in gold paint.

DIMIDIATION The practice whereby half of one coat of arms is impaled (see impalement) on a shield with half of another coat of arms.

DIMINUTIVE Smaller, often multiple, version of an ordinary or sub-ordinary.

EMBLAZON To draw or paint a coat of arms in full color.

ERASED Of a limb of a human being or creature, or any part of an entity, as if pulled off the main body, leaving a jagged edge.

ERECT Of any item, placed upright.

ERMINE Of the tinctures of heraldry, one of the furs; white with black "tails."

ESCUTCHEON A shield, usually small, used as a charge upon another.

ESCUTCHEON OF PRETENCE A small shield bearing the arms of an heiress placed upon the shield of her husband's arms.

ESTOILE A representation of a star, with six wavy points or rays.

FESSE A horizontal strip across the middle of the shield; an ordinary; ("per Fesse," the field divided horizontally into two equal parts; "in fess," charges placed on the shield in this position).

FESS-POINT The mid-point of shield.

FIELD The color that the shield is painted before anything is placed upon it, and the divisions of this, if more than one tincture is used.

FLEUR DE LYS  A stylized form of the lily, in many varieties. Widely used in French heraldry, particularly royal.

GOUTTE (GUTTE)  A small, drop-shaped figure of specified tincture, used as a charge.
GOUTTY  Covered with small, drop-shaped figures.
GRADY  Of a line of partition, stepped.
GRANT OF ARMS  A formal document giving sole right to a person and his heirs to bear arms, granted by a competent authority.
GRIFFIN (GRYPHON)  A mythical beast, having the head and wings of an eagle and the body and hind quarters of a lion.
GUARDANT  Of a creature or human, looking out of the shield at the observer.
GULES  Of the tinctures of heraldry, the color red.
GUNSTONE  A black roundel, also known as a pellate.
GYRON  A wedge-shaped charge, placed in the lower diagonal half of a canton.

HARPY  A monster, having a woman's face and body and a bird's wings and claws.
HATCHMENT  A diamond-shaped board with armorial bearings painted for the funeral of the bearer.
HEATER  A shape of shield, resembling a flat iron.
HELM  Heraldic term for a helmet.
HORNED  With horns, in a separate specified color.

IMPALEMENT  The practice of placing two, sometimes three, coats of arms side by side on the same shield.
INCENSED  Issuing flames or vapor.
INCRESCENT  Of a crescent, facing dexter.
INDENTED  Of a line of partition, having a series of similar indentations or notches.
INVERTED  Of a winged creature, with the wings open, the tips downward.

JESSANT DE LYS  Of a face, placed before a fleur de lys with the lower part of the fleur thrust out through the mouth.

JESSED  Of the jesses tying a bell to a falcon's leg, in a separate specified color.
JOUSTING  Organized combat between mounted knights for pageantry, display, prowess, and training.

KING OF ARMS  The senior herald in a country.
KNIGHT  One elevated to this rank and admitted to one of the orders of knighthood by the competent authority in recognition of deeds of valor or great service; a non-hereditary rank; "Ritter" in Germany, "chevalier" in France.

LAMBREQUIN  Synonymous with mantling.
LANGUED  Of the tongue, in a separate specified color.
LEAVED  Of the leaves of a plant, in a separate color.
LINE OF PARTITION  Lines drawn to delineate divisions and charges can be of many different configurations.
LIONCEL  A small lion, used to describe one of many on one shield.
LIVERY  The uniform worn by a lord's retainers, bearing his colors.
LOZENGE  A diamond-shaped piece.
LOZENGY  Of an all-over lozenge pattern, made by crossing diagonal lines.

MANTLING  A short cloth attached to the back of the helmet to keep off the sun's heat and protect against sword cuts.
MANDRAKE  A human monster, formed from the root of the plant of the same name.
MARSHALING  The practice of combining two or more coats of arms on a shield or in one achievement.
MARTLET  A bird of the swift order, shown with no feet.
METAL  Of the tinctures of heraldry, the colors that represent silver and gold.
MILL-RIND  Iron bracket to take the spindle in the center of a millstone to prevent wear.
MOLLET (MULLET)  A five-pointed star shape, not to be confused with a star; when pierced representing a spur rowel.

MOON  Shown either full, with a human face, to differentiate it from a plate or as a crescent. See also increscent and decrescent.

NAIANT  Of fish, swimming across the shield, heads to the dexter.

NAVEL POINT  The lower middle point of a shield, below the fess point.

NEBULY  Of a line of partition, of a wavy or serpentine form.

NOWED  Knotted, of a rope, a tail, a snake, etc.

OCTOFOIL  A flower with eight petals.

OGRESS  A black roundel, synonymous with gunstone.

OR  Of the tinctures representing metals, the color gold.

ORDINARY  The principal geometric charge on a shield.

OUNCE  A mythical beast resembling a leopard, in heraldry often a black panther.

PAIRLE  A division of the field into three radiant sections.

PALE  An ordinary, being a vertical stripe or band in the middle of the shield.

PALY  Of the field, divided into an equal number of vertical strips.

PALY BENDY  Of the field, divided into sections by vertical and diagonal lines.

PASSANT  Of a creature, walking across the shield.

PASSION CROSS  One of the forms of the cross; the standard crucifix.

PEAN  One of the heraldic tinctures that represent the furs, black with gold spots.

PENNON  A small pointed flag fixed at the lance point.

PEON  A broad arrowhead with the inside edge serrated.

POTENTY  Of a line of partition, formed by a series of potents, or crutch heads.

PROPER  Of anything in heraldry blazoned in its natural color.

PURPURE  Of the tinctures of heraldry, purple.

QUARTER  The top dexter quarter on a shield.

QUARTERING  One of any number of divisions on a shield, on which are placed different coats of arms.

QUATREFOIL  A stylized flower with four petals, representing the poppy.

QUEUE FOURCHY  Of the forked tail of a creature.

QUILLED  Of the shaft of a feather, synonymous with "penned."

RAMPANT  Of a creature, reared up to fight.

RAYONNE  A line of partition, having alternating pointed projections and depressions with wavy edges.

ROUNDEL  A circle, of various colors, each having its own name.

SABLE  Of the heraldic tinctures, the color black.

SAGITTARY  A human monster, having the body of a lion joined to the torso of a man.

SALIENT  Of a creature, leaping.

SALTIRE  An ordinary, two crossed strips across the shield, diagonally.

SANGUINE  Of the tinctures of heraldry one of the stains, dark blood-red.

SEAL  A tool with an heraldic device carved upon it, used to make an impression in wax, as a sign of authenticity; the wax impression itself. Synonymous with garb.

SHIELD  The main defensive item of a man fighting on foot or horseback, used to ward off offensive blows. Nowadays the main item on which to display armorial bearings.

SINISTER  Left, considered from the point of view of the person bearing the shield, thus standing behind it.

STAINS  Colors of the tinctures of heraldry that are not primary colors.

STATANT  Of a creature, simply standing, facing the dexter.

STANDARD  A long flag with a partly colored fringe, now displaying the arms, crest, motto, and livery colors of the bearer.

STAR  In heraldry represented as a figure with six wavy arms, called an estoile; with five points it is called a mollet.

SUB-ORDINARY  Any one of a group of the smaller, less frequently used, geometric shapes found as charges.

SUNBURST  A cloud with the sun's rays issuant.

SUN IN SPLENDOR  The sun, issuing rays.

SUPPORTER  Any creature holding up a shield or helm, most commonly in pairs.

TALBOT  A large hunting dog with drooping ears, the model for representations of a hunting dog in heraldry.

TENNÉ (TENNY)  Of the tinctures of heraldry, one of the stains, tawny orange.

TIARA  Usually refers in heraldry to the papal headpiece of three crowns.

TINCTURE  In heraldry the term for all the colors employed.

TILTING SPEAR  Special spear used in tournaments.

TOMB EFFIGY  A prone statue of the deceased placed upon his tomb.

TORSE  A twist of material covering the joint between crest and helm, synonymous with "wreath."

TRANSFIXED  Pierced by a weapon.

TRICK  A shorthand way of noting down a blazon.

TRICORPORATE  Of a creature, having one head and three bodies.

TRIPPANT (TRIPPING)  Of deer, trotting or walking across the shield to the dexter, with one paw raised.

TUFTED  Of creatures, having tufts of hair on their knees, elbows, flanks, shoulders, or chin.

TUDOR ROSE  An heraldic rose, composed of a white rose charged upon a red rose, reversed, if placed upon a red field; occasionally found quartered and countercharged, plain quartered or parted per pale.

TYGER  An heraldic creature, bearing little resemblance to a real tiger.

UNDY  Of a line of partition, wavy.

UNGULED  Of the hoofs of a creature, in a separate specified color.

UNICORN  Fabulous horse monster with horn.

URCHIN  A hedgehog.

URDY  Of a line of partition, pointing, having points.

URINANT  Of a fish, swimming down to the bottom of the shield.

VAIR  Of the tinctures in heraldry, one of the furs, (blue and white).

VAIRY  Of a field of the vair type, but of specified tincture.

VALLARY CROWN  An heraldic crown; from the Roman tradition of bestowing a crown on the first to mount an enemy's rampart).

VAMBRACED  Of an arm, protected by armor.

VERT  Of the tinctures of heraldry, one of the colors, green.

VISOR  The opening front of a helmet.

VOIDED  Of a charge, appearing in outline only.

VOLANT  Of a bird, flying across the shield with wings expanded.

VULNED  Wounded and bleeding.

WATTLED  Of a cock or other fowl, with skin hanging from the chin.

WAVY  Of lines of partition.

WOODWOSE (WOODHOUSE)  A wild man of the woods, used as a charge and sometimes as a supporter.

WREATH  See torse.

WREATHY  Of a sub-ordinary, depicted as if made like a wreath, with twists of cloth of various colors.

WYVERN (WIVERN)  A mythical beast, being a winged dragon with two eagle-like feet and a barbed, serpentine tail.

YALE An heraldic beast with horns and tusks.

# Further Reading

Bedingfeld, H. and Gwynn-Jones, P. *Heraldry*. London: Magna Books, 1993.

*Boutell's Heraldry*, revised by J.P. Brooke-Little. London: Frederick Warne & Co. Ltd., 1983.

Dennys, Rodney. *The Heraldic Imagination*. New York: Clarkson N. Potter, Inc., 1975.

Fox-Davies, A. C. *A Complete Guide to Heraldry*. New York: Dodge Publishing Co., 1909. Reprinted —New York: Bonanza Books, 1978. Revised by J.P. Brooke-Little, New York: Bonanza Books, 1985. Paperback printing: Wordsworth Editions Ltd, 1999.

Fox-Davies, A. C. *The Art of Heraldry*. London: Bloomsbury Books, 1986.

Franklyn, Julian. *Shield & Crest*. London: MacGibbon & Kee, 1960. Revised edition, 1967.

Friar, S. and Ferguson, J. *Basic Heraldry*. London: Herbert Press, 1993.

Galbreath, Donald L. and Léon Jéquier. *Manuel du Blason*. Lausanne, 1977.

Innes of Learney, Sir Thomas. *Scots Heraldry*. 1st Ed: 1934. 2nd Ed, Edinburgh: Oliver and Boyd, 1956. Reprint: Baltimore Publishing Co., 1971. 3d edition revised by Sir Malcolm Innes of Edingight, Edinburgh: Johnston and Bacon, 1978.

Moncreiffe, Iain, and Don Pottinger. *Simple Heraldry*, 2nd ed. Edinburgh: John Bartholomew and Son Limited, 1978.

Neubecker, Ottfried. *Heraldry: Sources, Symbols and Meaning*. Maidenhead: McGraw-Hill Book Co. (UK) Limited, 1976.

Pastoureau, Michel. *Heraldry: its origins and meaning*. London: Thames and Hudson, 1997.

Pine, Leslie Gilbert: *Heraldry, Ancestry and Titles: Questions and Answers*. New York: Gramercy Publishing Co, 1965.

Pine, Leslie Gilbert: *International Heraldry*. New York: Gramercy Publishing Co, 1965.

Rothery, Guy Cadogan. *An ABC of Heraldry*. London: Stanley Paul, 1915. Reprinted as *Concise Encyclopaedia of Heraldry*. London: Bracken Books, 1985.

Slater, Stephen. *The Illustrated Book of Heraldry*. London: Hermes House, Anness Publishing Ltd, 2002. Reprinted 2006.

Volborth, Carl-Alexander von. *Heraldry—Customs, Rules and Styles*. Poole: Blandford Press, 1981.

Volborth, Carl-Alexander von. *Heraldry of the World*. Poole: Blandford Press, 1973.

Woodcock, Thomas, and John Martin Robinson. *The Oxford Guide to Heraldry*. Oxford: Oxford University Press, 1988. Paperback edition, 1990.

Woodward, John, and George A. Burnett. *A Treatise on Heraldry British and Foreign, with English and French Glossaries*. Originally published 1891. Reprinted 1969, with new introduction by L.G. Pine, Rutland (Vermont): Charles E Tuttle Co., and Newton Abbot: David & Charles Reprints, 1969.

Zieber, Eugene. *Heraldry in America*. Philadelphia, 1895. Repr. 1977, Genealogical Publishing Co. 1984, New York; Greenwhich House.

# INDEX

# ACKNOWLEDGMENTS

## PICTURE CREDITS

The British Library: pp 21, 26, 27, 29.

Cognizance Heraldic Artwork Agency: pp 78, 107, 110, 145, 174–5, 176, 181, 183 bottom right.

Dover Publications: pp 84, 125 top, 191 bottom left and right.

E. T. Archive: pp 2, 13, 40, 43, 44, 47, 57, 58, 60–61, 79, 85, 101, 121, 171.

Clive Hicks: pp 7, 8, 9, 13 top, 17, 114, 139, 160, 161.

Fernand Nathan: pg 119.

A. F. Kersting: pp 117, 118, 166, 182, 201, 202, 129.

Musée Condé, Chantilly: pg 19.

National and Historical Symbols of Hungary: pp 45, 130.

Shutterstock: pp 5, 10, 20, 25, 27, 28, 34, 37, 38, 44 left, 51, 52 bottom right, 54, 80, 81, 83, 86, 87, 95, 99, 103, 108, 111, 113, 115, 116, 130, 132, 133 bottom, 134, 136, 137 bottom right, 144 bottom left, 151 top, 152, 159, 163, 164, 165, 170, 172, 173, 177 top right, 179, 184 bottom, 185, 190, 191 top (Semen Lixodeev), 194, 196, 203, 208, 213.

University of Newcastle: pg 31

Wikimedia Commons: pp 91, 93, 153, 193, 195.

## AUTHOR'S ACKNOWLEDGMENTS

The author wishes to thank Marie Neal for her untiring and patient help in preparing this book, and the Cognizance Heraldic Artwork Agency for permission to reproduce photographs of the work of contemporary heraldic craftsmen. Thanks are also due to all those who have offered help and criticism, and to Lorraine Greenoak who precipitated the whole project.